S.J. PEPLOE

S.J. PEPLOE

Alice Strang, Elizabeth Cumming and Frances Fowle

National Galleries of Scotland
Edinburgh 2012

Published by the Trustees of the National Galleries of
Scotland to accompany the exhibition, *S.J. Peploe*, held at the
Scottish National Gallery of Modern Art, Edinburgh, from
3 November 2012 to 23 June 2013.

Exhibition curated by Alice Strang
Research by Rachel Smith, Doughty Hanson Assistant Curator
Text © The Trustees of the National Galleries of Scotland 2012

ISBN 978 1 906270 51 3   paperback
ISBN 978 1 906270 58 2   hardback

Designed and typeset in Arnhem by Dalrymple
Printed on Perigord 150gsm by die Keure, Belgium

Front cover: detail from *The Coffee Pot* [22]
Back cover: detail from *Landscape, South of France* [84]
Frontispiece: detail from *Self-portrait* [24]

The proceeds from the sale of this book go towards
supporting the National Galleries of Scotland. For a
complete list of current publications, please write to NGS
Publishing, Scottish National Gallery of Modern Art,
75 Belford Road, Edinburgh EH4 3DR, or visit our website:
www.nationalgalleries.org

National Galleries of Scotland is a charity registered in
Scotland (no.SC003728)

NATIONAL
GALLERIES
SCOTLAND

CONTENTS

SPONSOR'S FOREWORD

Dickson Minto ws, established in 1985, is a leading multinational practice law firm providing corporate and commercial legal services to national and international clients. With offices in London and Edinburgh, the firm is committed to delivering the highest standard of service to all clients whether small, medium or large, private or public. We also have a high regard for the visual arts and are delighted to be sponsoring the exhibition *S.J. Peploe*, following upon our first sponsorship with the National Galleries of Scotland of the exhibition *F.C.B. Cadell*. Of the group of artists known as the Scottish Colourists, Peploe is the most well known, perhaps above all for his beautiful still lifes of the 1920s. Equally enduring are his touching portraits of his family and his evocative depictions of the north end of Iona and the south of France. The oldest of the Colourists, Peploe had a huge influence on the others, particularly Cadell, and it seems particularly fitting that we support this exhibition.

We are especially pleased to be associated with this very important third retrospective of the artist by the National Galleries of Scotland as the firm's Edinburgh offices are located in Charlotte Square, where Peploe attended school before being apprenticed as a solicitor.

We know that this exhibition will give enormous pleasure to every visitor and we are delighted to have had the opportunity to support it. We look forward to extending our relationship with the National Galleries of Scotland for many years to come.

DIRECTORS' FOREWORD

This book accompanies the third retrospective exhibition of the work of Samuel John Peploe to be staged by the National Galleries of Scotland; the first, curated by the Galleries' then Director, Stanley Cursiter, was held in 1941. The second, curated by the artist's grandson, Guy Peploe, was held in 1985. The time is therefore ripe to reassess Peploe's achievements.

The exhibition is the second in a series of retrospectives dedicated to the work of three of the four artists popularly known as the Scottish Colourists. In 2011 we examined the significance of F.C.B. Cadell and we shall do the same for J.D. Fergusson in 2013. (G.L. Hunter was the subject of a major exhibition at the City Art Centre in Edinburgh in 2012.) Peploe was the eldest and most successful – commercially and critically – of the four and was the social lynchpin of the group.

Since his first solo exhibition, held in Edinburgh in 1903, the beauty and importance of Peploe's work has been recognised and it can be found in many public as well as private collections. Our thanks are due to all the lenders to the exhibition, without whose generosity this project would have been impossible. We are particularly grateful to Aberdeen Art Gallery & Museums Collections and to Fife Council Museums: Kirkcaldy Museum & Art Gallery, for lending so freely from their holdings of Peploe's paintings. We are indebted to many others who have facilitated loans and helped with research, in particular Peploe's descendants and those of his patrons. Special thanks are due to Guy Peploe, whose monograph on his grandfather has recently been re-published and who has contributed a preface to this publication. As Managing Director of The Scottish Gallery, who represented Peploe throughout his career, Guy has helped as much with professional as with academic and biographical matters. Furthermore, with his family, Guy has presented an important tranche of archival material relating to Peploe to the Scottish National Gallery of Modern Art, on the occasion of this exhibition.

Before his untimely death, Nigel Doughty kindly agreed to fund a post to support the Peploe project, through the British private equity firm which he co-founded. Rachel Smith was thus appointed the Doughty Hanson Assistant Curator and has ably assisted Alice Strang, curator of the exhibition. We would like to thank all of their colleagues at the National Galleries of Scotland who have been involved with the realisation of this venture. Alice, Frances Fowle and Elizabeth Cumming have contributed illuminating essays to this publication.

Particular thanks are also due to: Roger Billcliffe of The Roger Billcliffe Gallery; Patrick and Cordelia Bourne of The Fine Art Society; Alistair Drennan; Duncan Miller of Duncan R. Miller Fine Arts; Ewan and Carol Mundy of Ewan Mundy Fine Art; Peter and Renate Nahum; Susannah Pollen of Susannah Pollen Ltd; and Selina Skipwith of The Fleming Collection. At the auction houses we are grateful to Chris Brickley of Bonhams; Bernard Williams and André Zlattinger of Christie's; Campbell Armour of Lyon & Turnbull; Charlotte Canby of Shapes Auctioneers; and Michael Grist of Sotheby's. Our research has been greatly helped by: Margaret Drew Bongiovanni, Furman University, Greenville; David Devereux, The Stewartry Museum, Kirkcudbright; Jane MacAvock; Dr Lorn Macintyre; Philip MacLeod Coupe; David Mitchell, Curator – Projects, Royal Botanic Garden, Edinburgh; and Bill Smith.

Finally, we are thrilled that in continuation of their support of the National Galleries of Scotland and following their sponsorship of our Cadell exhibition, Dickson Minto ws have generously agreed to sponsor the Peploe exhibition.

JOHN LEIGHTON
Director-General, National Galleries of Scotland

SIMON GROOM
Director, Scottish National Gallery of Modern Art

[1] S.J. Peploe, *c.*1920

Private collection, courtesy The Scottish Gallery, Edinburgh

PREFACE

GUY PEPLOE

S.J. Peploe was born in the year Stanley met Livingstone; the year of the Paris Commune and two months before the first ever rugby international match was settled with a 4–1 win for Scotland over England, also in Edinburgh. He married late and so did his second son, my father Denis, so that I was not destined to know my grandfather; but I feel as if I did. I think he would have been a splendid grandfather, shy to the point of appearing austere to the outside world, but a warm, family man full of fun and surprises. He would have been proud of his children and their children's accomplishments and indulgent of how my enthusiasm and regard for his art has developed into a large part of my own career. He was certainly not indifferent to how he was thought of as a painter; he knew he was good, but the fuss and personal attention which comes with national and international recognition would only have been superficially welcome: he was intensely private and would tend to retreat rapidly if the subject turned to himself.

Any artist making his way in the century of Modernism can suffer the fate of 'temporary relevance' as the complex history of the period is refined and approved by succeeding art historians and curators, particularly when the artist is associated with the origin of a modernist movement. Peploe, however, was recognised in his lifetime as an original painter in each phase of his development, although hostility and incomprehension were familiar accompanists. When the Scottish Modern Arts Association convened for their inaugural meeting in 1907, to choose contemporary pictures for a National Collection, the choice of a Peploe of bananas painted in his most dashing, fluid, early style was controversial: what was worthy about a bunch of bananas? Peploe had already understood the modernist credo that any subject was legitimate, or – better – the subject for modern art was irrelevant. Within three years he had turned his back on his earlier accomplishments in favour of a full engagement with European Modernism and two decades of experiment.

For Peploe there was no objective beyond hard work and the idea that the next picture was the most important. The small scale of his pictures speaks of a lack of competitiveness: he painted for himself and found sufficient intellectual challenge at his easel and stimulation from a long walk. His lifelong attempt to reconcile a powerful, personal response to nature with rigour in composition places him closer to both Matisse and Mondrian than to any British painter, and firmly in the European avant-garde: his pictures were quietly acquired by several national and municipal collections whose curators recognised Peploe as a standard-bearer for British post-impressionist painting.

There was certainly a falling away of interest in Peploe in the decades after his death, but the reappraisal of the last thirty years is on firm foundations. I curated an exhibition for the Scottish National Gallery of Modern Art, the first in the converted Watson's College, in 1985 and then wrote a book which came out at around the same time as Philip Long's excellent *The Scottish Colourists 1900–1930* exhibition, shown at the same gallery after being launched at the Royal Academy of Arts, London in the year 2000. This new exhibition is of more significance as it comes as one of a series featuring some of Scotland's most important twentieth-century painters; a new edition of my book will complement Alice Strang's catalogue.

Today we can also see the thousand or so pictures Peploe made as a contribution to Scotland's cultural identity: strong, well-made and original works of art that remain present in our consciousness as if the independence of mind and intellectual probity characteristic of the Scottish Enlightenment had been put to use to serve the visual splendour of Scotland's environment. With typical modesty he said shortly before his death, aged only sixty-four, that if he had another ten years he might do something significant. This may be a regret for us all but does not diminish what he had already achieved.

1 · INTRODUCTION:
PEPLOE AND THE SCOTTISH COLOURISTS

ALICE STRANG

S.J. PEPLOE is invariably associated with the Scottish Colourists, along with F.C.B. Cadell (1883–1937), J.D. Fergusson (1874–1961) and G.L. Hunter (1877–1931), and is often acknowledged as their figure-head. Indeed, a review of the first exhibition of the work of all four to be held in London declared:

The four Scotsmen, of whom Mr Peploe may be considered the leader, are artists of pronounced individuality, with just sufficient in common to justify their being formed into a group. The connecting link is a bold emphasis of colour ... and a very modern synthetic simplification of form.[1]

There are affinities within the group, not least ex-tended periods spent in France, an early understand-ing of the work of developments in French painting from Manet and the Impressionists to Cézanne, Matisse and the Fauves and a love of brilliant colour. However, the four artists only exhibited together three times during their lifetimes and they never formed an official association with each other. The term 'Scottish Colourist' was not applied to them exclusively until 1948, when all but Fergusson had died.[2] Rather, the idea of linking their work was motivated by com-mercial interests and was promoted by the art dealer Alexander Reid and his son A.J. McNeill Reid.

Peploe was the eldest of the four artists. T.J. Honeyman, who knew Peploe through his posi-tion at the artist's Glasgow dealers Reid & Lefèvre, described him thus:

His manner was a little aloof. He was shy and protected himself with a shell. In casual conversation he wasted no words, his comments were dry and completely sincere, or if he had nothing to say he remained silent. ... He had a particular horror of 'arty'

people or any form of pretentiousness, and he avoided like the plague what he called 'overwhelmingly capable women'.[3]

However, Peploe had a talent for friendship and it was his relationships with his fellow Colourists that really binds them together. He met Fergusson first, around 1900, possibly in the studio club run by Joseph Simpson in Edinburgh.[4] By this point both men had studied in Edinburgh and Paris and established them-selves in studios in the Scottish capital, but neither had yet had a solo exhibition. They were particularly close before the First World War, especially between 1910 and 1912 when they lived in Paris. Their friend-ship lasted until Peploe's death in 1935, and Fergusson remembered it as:

A happy unbroken friendship between two painters who both believed that painting was not just a craft or profession, but a sustained attempt at finding a means of expressing reactions to life in the form demanded by each new experience.[5]

Peploe next became friends with Cadell, and his first recorded reference to the younger artist is in a let-ter of March 1909 to his future wife Margaret Mackay; both had their second solo exhibitions that year, at The Scottish Gallery.[6] Cadell remained in Edinburgh when Peploe moved to Paris, but they stayed in touch. During Cadell's war service Peploe frequently wrote to him, keeping him abreast, amongst other things, of developments in Fergusson's work.[7] The pair were at their closest following Cadell's demobilisation in the spring of 1919, and throughout the 1920s their homes and studios were within easy walking distance in Edinburgh. In 1920 Cadell introduced Peploe to the Hebridean island of Iona, where they returned to paint

[2] Detail from *Old Tom Morris,* late 1890s [33]

almost annually throughout the decade. Their friendship was, in the words of Honeyman, 'a rare thing. In appearance, manner and talk they were poles apart, but in their love of colour, sunshine and freedom of action they were on common ground.'[8]

According to Peploe's friend the artist E.A. Taylor, Hunter tried unsuccessfully to meet Peploe for the first time in Paris just before the outbreak of war; however, they were in touch by 1918.[9] Hunter could rely upon Peploe's honesty and McNeill Reid advised him to seek Peploe's opinion of his work, writing: 'do not be led astray by all the nice things your friends say about your work … get Peploe to be absolutely candid and you should then be able to find out their merits and defects.'[10] The pair remained friends until Hunter's death in 1931.

Of the Scottish Colourists, Peploe was the most successful professionally, in commercial and critical terms. From early in his career, he had the support of the two most influential dealers in Scotland: The Scottish Gallery in Edinburgh (part of the gilding and picture restoring firm Aitken Dott & Co.) and Alexander Reid's La Société des Beaux-Arts in Glasgow. His first solo exhibition with The Scottish Gallery was in 1903 and his first at Reid's in 1915. Between 1921 and 1927 one or two shows of his work were held each year in Edinburgh or Glasgow, or both, invariably accompanied by healthy sales. Peploe sent regularly to the Royal Scottish Academy (RSA) from 1896 until 1935 and to the Royal Glasgow Institute of the Fine Arts (RGI) from 1896 until 1934. He also sent to the Society of Scottish Artists (SSA) between 1897 and 1919 and again in 1930.

Peploe exhibited in London for the first time in 1907, in two exhibitions at the Baillie Gallery, at the Goupil Gallery and in the inaugural exhibition of the Allied Artists Association. After the amalgamation of Reid's and the Lefèvre Gallery in 1926 to form Alex Reid & Lefèvre, Peploe's work was shown regularly in the firm's London gallery as well. Indeed, the Reids did much to promote Peploe's work beyond Scotland after the war, organising solo and group exhibitions in London, Paris and New York and both they and The Scottish Gallery staged memorial exhibitions. Apart from his 1903 solo exhibition, Peploe stayed at one remove from commercial dealings, allowing his agents to select the work to be displayed and sold.

In group exhibitions, Peploe habitually appeared first in the list of exhibitors and was singled out for praise by critics. When reviewing the 1923 Leicester Galleries exhibition of the work of Peploe, Cadell and Hunter, *The Times* declared 'the most learned of the three is Mr Peploe: his design is full of cunning and his painting of mass and volume very powerful. He … loves strong colour and plays many fine fantasies with it.'[11] His solo exhibitions were also well covered in the press. The *Glasgow Herald* wrote of his 1924 solo exhibition at La Société des Beaux-Arts: 'If the modernity of Mr Peploe's art may have been at an earlier stage of his career somewhat disconcerting … there can be no doubt that his supreme powers as a colourist are now generally recognised and appreciated … the flower pictures – mostly roses set in Chinese porcelain vases – are highly decorative and very charming.'[12] Indeed the sheer number of related still lifes based on roses which Peploe painted in the period roughly between 1918 and 1923, combined with their commercial success, has distorted the understanding of Peploe's work and achievements.[13] His career is actually remarkable for its continual experimentation. None of the other Colourists exhibited with such regularity and prominence, received such uniform praise or achieved such dependable sales. However, Peploe was never a rich man. He lived with his family in a modest tenement flat in India Street, albeit in the heart of Edinburgh's Georgian New Town, from their return from Paris in 1912 until his death, and worried about paying his sons' Edinburgh Academy fees.[14]

Of the Scottish Colourists, Peploe's work was the first to be acquired for a public collection, when *Still Life* of *c*.1906 [3] was one of the original four works purchased by the Scottish Modern Arts Association in 1907. By the time of his death, Peploe was represented in public collections in Australia, England, France, Northern Ireland and Scotland.[15] He is now represented in the Scottish national collection by thirty-four paintings and four drawings. To this day, Peploe has the highest profile of the four Scottish Colourists, to each of whom he was a dear friend.

NOTE: *Although Peploe usually signed his works, he very rarely dated them. When paintings can be identified in exhibition lists or from other archival sources, dates are given. However, as so many were given generic titles such as* Still Life *or* Iona, *in most cases approximate dates are suggested. Dimensions are in centimetres, height before width.*

[3]

*Still Life, c.*1906

Oil on panel, 26.7 × 34.8
City Art Centre, City of Edinburgh Museums and Galleries,
presented by the Scottish Modern Arts Association, 1964

2 · 'I CAN NEVER SEE MYSTERY COMING TO AN END': A LIFE OF S.J. PEPLOE

ALICE STRANG

IN 1929, PEPLOE WROTE: 'There is so much in mere objects, flowers, leaves, jugs, what not – colours, forms, relation – I can never see mystery coming to an end.'[1] He thus summarised his lifelong interest in painting the genre of the still life. Indeed, Peploe is most celebrated for his still lifes, but of equal significance are the landscapes that he painted throughout his career, usually *en plein air*, and at certain periods he also created figure studies of beauty and significance. Peploe's talent was recognised from his first solo exhibition, held at The Scottish Gallery in Edinburgh in 1903. This early success makes his subsequent development all the more remarkable. Rather than simply continuing in this and later successful veins, Peploe persistently experimented with theory, style and technique. By the time of his death in 1935 and the subsequent memorial exhibitions of his work, Peploe was recognised as one of Scotland's most important modern artists, with a growing international reputation.

Samuel John Peploe was born on 27 January 1871 at 39 Manor Place, Edinburgh. His father, Robert Luff Peploe (1827–1884), was Assistant Secretary of the Commercial Bank of Scotland and had become its Manager by the time of his death [5]. His mother, Annie Hickock Peploe (née Watson) (1834–1874), was Peploe's father's second wife [6]. Peploe was the second of their three children, born between William Watson Peploe (1869–1933) and Annie Margaret Peploe (1874–1943) [7]; they had a half-brother from their father's first marriage, James Reid Peploe (1861–1935), who became a Major in the Duke of Edinburgh's Own Edinburgh Artillery Militia.

Peploe was three years old when his mother died and thirteen when his father died. He and his siblings were left in the care of eight trustees and were brought up by Mary Sanderson (1837–1914), whom they called 'Nannie' and who remained with the family until her death. Peploe went to Edinburgh Collegiate School and stated that he attended Edinburgh University, although no records exist to prove this. He tried various career options before deciding to become an artist, summing up this period in his life as 'thought in turns of being a soldier, minister, indigo planter, lawyer, farmer and other pursuits, but preferred doing nothing as long as possible'.[2]

Peploe began his art training at the age of twenty, dividing his time between Paris and Edinburgh. In Paris, he studied at the Académie Julian at various points between 1891 and 1894, under William-Adolphe Bouguereau (1825–1905), whom he described as a 'damned old fool' [9].[3] Whilst in Edinburgh, Peploe attended classes at the Life School of the RSA between 1892 and 1896 [8]. He became friends with the celebrated Aberdonian portraitist Robert Brough (1872–1905), with whom he returned to study in Paris, and was awarded the Maclaine Watters Medal in 1895. Peploe's brother-in-law, Dr Frederick Porter, recalled Sir George Reid, then President of the RSA, attending one of the classes:

> *Looking at Peploe's drawing he asked him when he was going to take his art seriously. Peploe turned round and asked Sir George if he would not like to be able to draw like that! Peploe was sure of himself from the beginning.*[4]

He began his professional career in 1896, taking on his first studio in the Albert Buildings at 24 Shandwick Place, Edinburgh. The painter and curator Stanley Cursiter (1887–1976), Peploe's friend and biographer, described it as:

[4] Detail from *Royan, Charente Inférieure*, 1910 [51]

[5] Robert Luff Peploe

Private collection, courtesy
The Scottish Gallery,
Edinburgh

[6] Annie Hickock Peploe

Private collection, courtesy
The Scottish Gallery,
Edinburgh

[7] Sam, Annie and
Willie Peploe, 1880

Private collection, courtesy
The Scottish Gallery,
Edinburgh

[8] The Royal Scottish
Academy Life Class,
session 1892–3. S.J. Peploe
is in the back row, fourth
from left. Robert Brough
is in the front row on the
far right.

Royal Scottish Academy
Collections

a large rambling building with, on its upper floors, rooms facing north, let as studios. These rooms had high windows or sloping roof lights ... Other rooms in the building were occupied by music teachers, elocutionists, offices and small businesses – a hive of industry enlivened by the scale passages of practising vocalists or the scraping of fiddles.[5]

In the same year Peploe exhibited with the RSA and RGI for the first time; his first submission to the SSA followed a year later.

As Frances Fowle discusses in her essay, during this period Peploe was interested in the French painter Édouard Manet (1832–1883), whose work he would have been able to see in Paris. He was also inspired by seventeenth-century Dutch Old Masters, in particular Frans Hals (*c*.1580/85–1666) and Rembrandt van Rijn (1606–1669). Peploe would have been familiar with Hals's *A Dutch Gentleman* and *A Dutch Lady* and with Rembrandt's *A Woman in Bed*, which were acquired by the National Gallery of Scotland (now the Scottish National Gallery) in 1885 and 1892 respectively. In 1895 or 1896 Peploe visited Holland and Cursiter later wrote: 'he returned excited and enthusiastic about the pictures he had seen and with a collection of

photographs and reproductions. There was always a reproduction or photograph of some picture by Rembrandt, Hals or Manet pinned to the walls of his studio.'[6]

This interest is borne out in Peploe's work of the late 1890s, as seen in *Gipsy* [18] and the unusually large *Old Tom Morris* [33]. They are extremely accomplished paintings, especially for an artist who had only recently completed his training. The mastery in the handling of oil paint, dark backgrounds, subtle lighting, delicate depiction of flesh and low-toned palette bring the sitters alive, namely the flower girl Jeannie Blyth and vagabond Tom Morris. Blyth began modelling for Peploe aged about fifteen and continued to do so until some time after she married. According to Cursiter she was 'a wonderful model, her dark hair and rich colour and complete lack of self-consciousness allowed Peploe to paint many pictures'.[7] The 'genial clean-shaven and toothless' Morris, caught in the act of a 'high-pitched cackle of an old man's laughter' also sat for Peploe over several years.[8]

It was also during the 1890s that Peploe began to paint *en plein air*, on the Hebridean island of Barra and in North Berwick, a coastal town south of Edinburgh [19, 20]. In 1894 he travelled to Barra for the first time,

with his brother William and their friend the painter Robert Cowan Robertson (1863–1910), and Peploe returned several times over the next decade. It was during the first trip that Peploe met his future wife, Margaret Mackay (1873–1958) [11], who was probably working in the post office in Castlebay. Margaret was from Lochboisdale on nearby South Uist and was able to get a transfer to the post office on Frederick Street in Edinburgh in order to be closer to Peploe during their lengthy courtship. Their grandson, Guy Peploe has described her as 'a mature, calm Hebridean, tall and athletic, with long black hair and a serenity in her presence, which was reflected in her character and was to give emotional substance to the artist for the rest of his life'.[9]

North Berwick Sands of about 1896 [20] was painted with creamy oil paint in subdued colours, applied with a generously loaded brush, employing a freer, looser technique than that used in Peploe's contemporary studio paintings. *A Windy Day at Barra* [19] of 1903 shows how Peploe's style changed in the intervening years; brighter colours are used, and the brushstrokes are shorter, cruder and more vigorously applied, conveying a sense of immediacy and speed of execution in a depiction of Castlebay. It is painted on a panel which measures 24 × 29 centimetres, which would have fitted in one of Peploe's pochades. Wooden boxes with

handles making them easy to carry when working outdoors, these contain spaces for a palette, brushes and tubes of paint and a couple of panels, one of which could slot in so that still-wet surfaces were not spoilt.

In about 1900 Peploe moved studio to 7 Devon Place [10]. It was here that he began the series of exquisite still lifes with which he made his reputation, such as *Still Life, Painter's Materials* [23] and *The Lobster* [21]. In the former Peploe depicted the tools of his trade, including bottles of turpentine, tubes of oil paint and paintbrushes, endowing them with a poise and majesty which is also found in the more sophisticated subject matter of the latter. In a painting of startling simplicity, the lobster, lemon on white plate and bone-handled knife are set against a dark background which is barely distinguishable from the table on which they are placed. The unusual vertical signature is a gesture towards oriental calligraphy and is an integral part of the composition. The highlights of orange, yellow and white show the skilful use of colour which was to come to fruition in later work. *The Lobster* recalls the *bodegones* of Diego Velázquez (1599–1660), another artist whom Peploe held in high regard.[10]

Gradually, Peploe began to work on a larger scale and with a growing virtuosity, as seen in *The Coffee Pot* [22] and *The Black Bottle* (SNGMA). The narrative implications of their after-dinner atmosphere, the rich

[10] S.J. Peploe in his 7 Devon Place studio, *c.*1904
National Library of Scotland, Edinburgh

[11] Margaret Mackay, *c.*1900
Private collection, courtesy The Scottish Gallery, Edinburgh

paint applied with aplomb, the counterpoint of bright white tablecloth against dark background, the glint of light on silver and glass and the touches of bright colour in fruit and porcelain make these paintings the masterpieces of Peploe's early career. As Philip Long has explained: 'These still lifes were executed following Manet's technique, Peploe first painting in light areas and then adding darks and half-tones while the paint remained wet.'[11] These studio works are significantly different from the landscapes which Peploe was painting at roughly the same time in places like Comrie in Perthshire, where his sister was living following her marriage to Dr Frederick Porter, as Frances Fowle discusses in her essay.

It was during this period that Peploe embarked on a series of self-portraits, a genre to which he rarely returned. In the example in the Scottish National Portrait Gallery, he shows himself facing the viewer whilst smoking a pipe; wisps of smoke echo the ambiguous cream brushstroke at the upper left, the white of his collar enlivening the otherwise sombre palette [24]. Most attention is paid to the face, whilst the composition dissolves away in the lower quarter. A roughly contemporary photograph shows how accurate his depiction is [12].

By this point Peploe and John Duncan Fergusson had become friends. The normally reserved Peploe explained to Margaret:

With Fergusson I am bright and witty – I keep him in a continual state of laughter … Whenever we meet, I tell you, we have a really lively time. I know what he gets from me – I stimulate him, excite him. And I get from him a strength and a cheerfulness which when alone I do not possess.[12]

Peploe and Fergusson embarked on painting trips together, including to Islay in 1904. That year they also began annual summer visits to France which had a significant effect on their work and ultimately lead them both to move to Paris, Fergusson in 1907 and Peploe in 1910 [37].

In 1903, at the age of thirty-two, Peploe had his first solo exhibition. It was held at The Scottish Gallery in Edinburgh and the painstaking trouble he took over its preparation contrasts with the 'hands-off' approach he adopted thereafter to his exhibitions. He wrote to Margaret: 'Tomorrow I give the colours of the walls at ten, see catalogue proofs at eleven; at twelve back to the studio to receive frames; then there is the work of fixing canvases into them, nailing down etc. … I do wish it were all over, so that I might get back to my quiet work.'[13] The exhibition was a success, though not without controversy, and twenty works sold, including *Fruit Piece* which was bought by Fergusson for £15.[14] James Caw reviewed it in *The Studio*, declaring 'Mr Peploe's vision is not very subtle and he is possessed by a perverse taste for the ugly or the bizarre in figure and landscape' whilst also praising his 'remarkable virtuosity and power in paint'.[15]

Two years later, Peploe moved studio to 32 York Place. It had been built in 1795 for the leading Scottish portrait painter Henry Raeburn (1756–1823). Raeburn designed an unusually large window in the north-facing studio at the rear of the first floor, with views over the Firth of Forth to Fife. It was flanked by an intricate system of shutters which enabled the occupant to control the light that entered the room. Cursiter, who used the studio himself after the Second World War, explained: 'Peploe decorated the room in a pale grey with a hint of pink; on the floor he had a black polished linoleum, a white sofa, a few chairs, an antique bureau, an easel and a model's throne.'[16]

Peploe's new bright and spacious surroundings had an immediate impact on his work and he began to paint in a lighter key, employing a looser, less disciplined technique and large canvases. He continued painting still lifes, but using a new model, Peggy

[12] S.J. Peploe, *c*.1904
National Library of Scotland, Edinburgh

Macrae, he embarked on a series of celebrated figure studies, such as *Girl in White* [26], which reveal an interest in James McNeill Whistler (1834–1903). Cursiter described Macrae as 'a charming, witty and attractive girl, who had the rare gift of complete grace which made her every movement interesting; she dropped naturally into poses which were balanced and harmonious'.[17] In Peploe's images of Macrae, her elegance and beauty are secondary to the sense of execution, as he emphasised colour harmony and sweeping line at the expense of subject matter. As Guy Peploe has explained: 'Peploe later likened painting in oil to dancing: movements back and forward to the canvas, precision and control of gesture. There would always be tracks on his studio floor, like a fast bowler's run-up, where the artist had moved back to inspect and forward to paint.'[18] The portrait of *Mrs Peploe* [25] of about 1907 is an interesting transitional work, between the formal still lifes of Devon Place and the more freely painted depictions of Macrae.

Peploe's professional and personal success began to build in the period 1907 to 1910. In 1907, *Still Life* [3] became the first work of his to be acquired for a public collection, as one of the inaugural four purchases made by the Scottish Modern Arts Association. Its acquisition was met with some controversy, as it was considered avant-garde 'and, in any case, who wanted a picture of two bananas?'[19] The same year Peploe showed in London for the first time, in various group exhibitions, including at the Baillie Gallery, the Goupil Gallery and in the first exhibition of the Allied Artists Association. In March 1909 he held his second solo exhibition, once more at The Scottish Gallery. This time, however, its manager Peter McOmish Dott paid Peploe £450 in advance for sixty pictures and before the end of April Dott had sold thirty-six works for a total of £530.[20] Six works were purchased by the leading Glasgow-based dealer Alexander Reid, who began to promote Peploe in the west of Scotland.[21] By the end of the year Peploe had become friends with Francis Campbell Boileau Cadell. The following year, on discovering Margaret was pregnant, she and Peploe were finally married at Christ Church in Morningside, Edinburgh on 5 April.

Despite the success he had so far achieved, Peploe must have felt a need for a new direction. Encouraged by Fergusson who had moved to Paris three years earlier and enabled by the money he had received from Dott, the Peploes moved to France not long after their

[13] S.J. Peploe, Margaret and Willy, 278 boulevard Raspail, Paris, 1910
Private collection, courtesy The Scottish Gallery, Edinburgh

[14] 13 India Street, Edinburgh, Peploe's home from 1912 until his death. He lived on the second floor where the three windows on the left indicate his flat.

wedding. After his studies in Paris and painting trips to the Normandy coast with Fergusson, Peploe now embarked on a crucial two-year period of submersion in the latest developments in French art, and the possibilities they opened up within his studio and outdoor practice. His work underwent a dramatic change, as discussed by Frances Fowle.

The Peploes' first son, Willy, was born in Royan on 29 August 1910 and they shortly afterwards settled in a studio-apartment at 278 boulevard Raspail, Montparnasse, Paris [13]. Fergusson recalled this period in their lives:

> We were a very happy group: Anne Rice, Jo Davidson, Harry and Bill McColl, Yvonne and Louis de Kerstratt [sic], Roffy the poet, La Torrie, mathematician and aviator. Other good friends in the Quarter were E.A. Taylor and Jessie King, who made a link with the Glasgow School. We used to meet round the corner at Boudet's restaurant … When we couldn't pay we did our signed and dated portraits on the back of the bill. After dinner we went to L'Avenue for coffee and music. La Rotonde was then only a zinc with seats for three … We were all very excited with the Russian Ballet when it came to Paris. Bakst was a sociétaire of the Salon d'Automne and used all the ideas of modern painting in his décor. Diaghilev made a triumph, surely even greater than he had hoped for. No wonder S.J. [sic] said these were some of the greatest nights of his life. They were the greatest nights in anyone's life.[22]

Peploe became a *sociétaire* of the progressive Salon d'Automne and exhibited with them in 1911 and 1912. He continued to send to the RGI, RSA and SSA and returned to Edinburgh intermittently. During one such visit in April 1911, Peploe was taken by the contrast not only between Paris and Edinburgh, but also between his recent work and that which he was making before the move to France. He wrote to Margaret:

> I saw at Dott's some of my old sketches and some of the things he bought just before we married and they are damned good. … But all the same I like my Royan sketches a thousand times better. I think they are a tremendous advance.[23]

He continued:

> You are jolly lucky being in Paris – you've no idea how stupid and beastly it is here. Everyone is most kind, but I miss just the thing I get in Paris – the stir of life

and the gay brightness … There's nothing here but healthy-looking people with golf clubs.[24]

Given the inspiration Peploe found in Paris and the pace of development in his work, it is not clear why the family moved back to Edinburgh in 1912, but it was presumably for personal rather than professional reasons. They rented a second-floor flat at 13 India Street where they lived until their deaths; their second son, Denis, was born on 25 March 1914 [14].[25] Peploe established himself in a studio at 34 Queen Street, where he remained until 1917.

Peploe's new work was received with scorn in Edinburgh, whilst it was exhibited widely in London, raising the question of why the family did not settle in the English capital, as Fergusson chose to do on the outbreak of the First World War. T.J. Honeyman explained: 'McOmish Dott, in whom sincere friendship fought a losing battle with the equally sincere convictions of the art dealer, simply could not face the prospect of being associated in any way with the new, raucous, exuberant kind of painting.'[26] Undeterred, Peploe organised an exhibition of it himself at the New Gallery, 12 Shandwick Place, the premises of the Society of Eight, an exhibiting society co-founded by Cadell in 1912. Honeyman continued: 'It created some stir, but the general view was that Peploe had run off the rails and that it was better to wait until he had run on again … However, there were a few staunch supporters … and in due time … it was recognised that something new and worthwhile had happened to Scottish Art.'[27] Peploe did not exhibit at The Scottish Gallery again until 1922, but continued to send consistently to the RGI, RSA and SSA.

In contrast, Peploe's work was widely exhibited in London between 1912 and 1914. The Stafford Gallery mounted solo exhibitions first of paintings and then of drawings in 1912. Peploe, Fergusson and eight other artists were shown together in an exhibition of *The Rhythm Group* at the Stafford Gallery in October that year, and Peploe was included in a group exhibition of *Modern Pictures* at the Grosvenor Gallery in the same month. The Baillie Gallery gave Peploe a solo exhibition of fifty-eight works in March 1914, whilst he and Fergusson were selected for inclusion in the landmark exhibition of twentieth-century art held at the Whitechapel Art Gallery two months later. By this time, and following the abrupt change in his work, Peploe had once more been recognised, at least in some quarters, as one of the leading artists of his generation.

Peploe was forty-three when the First World War was declared. As Margaret recalled: 'He was called up for service but was rejected because of his very bad heart – and his eyesight. I was very thankful because I knew that Sam could never stand the severe training and winter under canvas.'[28] However lonely and difficult they were, the war years nevertheless proved to be a fruitful time of more experimentation. Peploe wrote to Cadell, by then serving in France:

> *I am finished for good with the colour block system that interested me for a long time and await a new development ... I feel isolated here alone, one just keeps going like a machine – I have to paint ... The price of paint is getting prohibitive – also scarce. Canvas almost unobtainable.*[29]

Several trips were made to Kirkcudbright, where E.A. Taylor (1874–1951) and Jessie M. King (1875–1949) had settled. King even persuaded the reticent Peploe to act as the Pied Piper, wearing a costume she designed, in the town pageant of 1918 [15]. In Kirkcudbright, Peploe applied the lessons he had learnt in Paris to the Scottish landscape. As Guy Peploe has commented on his paintings of the town: 'The stolid geometry of Kirkcudbright, its tollbooth, castle and harbour, provided inspiration and the type of subject-matter which lent itself well to the geometrical analysis which was still the artist's dominant concern. These works are also some of the last where colour is pushed beyond naturalism into the territory of fauvism.'[30] This can be seen in *Kirkcudbright* [29] of about 1918.

In the 34 Queen Street studio, Peploe 'surrounded himself with bright colours, lengths of material, flat boards distempered or painted in pure strong tints, the walls white-washed and the room kept as light as possible'.[31] Here he continued to develop the richly coloured, spatially compressed still lifes that he had embarked upon whilst in Paris. They are in stark contrast to the still lifes he painted before 1910 and are amongst the most remarkable paintings in British art of this period. Structure, design and pattern became more pronounced, as seen in *Still Life* [27] of about 1912. Peploe's work at this time was described in Scotland as cubist.[32] However, Peploe did not pursue abstraction as far as Pablo Picasso (1881–1973) and Georges Braque (1882–1963). A knowledge of the work

of Vincent van Gogh (1853–1890) became apparent, as seen in *Tulips and Fruit* [28], whose furrowed brush-strokes and pronounced outlines recall the Dutch artist's late work, which Peploe would have been able to see in Paris. In the ambitious *Flowers and Fruit (Japanese Background)* [30] a multi-layered composition culminates in the inclusion of a Japanese print, whilst the exploration of volume in the compotier of fruit points to an interest in the work of Paul Cézanne (1839–1906), which Elizabeth Cumming examines in her essay.

Peploe's professional reputation continued to grow during the war. In November 1915 he had his first solo exhibition at Alexander Reid's gallery, La Société des Beaux-Arts, in Glasgow. Thus began a long and productive relationship with the other most prominent commercial gallery in Scotland besides The Scottish Gallery. Works were purchased by the important collectors William McInnes, a Glasgow ship-builder and J.W. Blyth, the Kirkcaldy linen manufacturer.[33] Blyth went on to amass the most important private collection of work by Peploe, much of which is now in the collection of Kirkcaldy Museum & Art Gallery. Reid offered Peploe an assured income of £200 by

[15] S.J. Peploe in a Pied Piper costume designed by Jessie M. King, Kirkcudbright, 1918

Private collection, courtesy The Stewartry Museum, Kirkcudbright

[16] S.J. Peploe with Margaret and Denis on Iona, *c.*1925

Private collection, courtesy The Scottish Gallery, Edinburgh

undertaking to buy pictures to that value each year, but even in the face of the poor state of the wartime art market, Peploe did not accept, preferring to retain his independence.[34]

In March 1918, Peploe was elected an Associate of the RSA, having been unsuccessfully proposed in 1909, thus finally receiving official approval from the Scottish art establishment. This was met with some reservation within the art world and by himself. When announcing his appointment *The Scotsman* described his work as 'strongly individual', and Peploe declared:

> *I know now that if there are chains of bondage there are also chains of love. Real freedom is being bound. Giving oneself up to a purpose, an idea, something greater than self.*[35]

The green light which reflected into his Queen Street studio from the trees across the road prompted Peploe to move studio in 1917 to 54 Shandwick Place. This was to prove his studio of longest standing and he remained there until 1934.[36] It had previously been occupied by James Paterson (1854–1932) and was close to Peploe's very first studio at no.24. This, the end of the war and the demobilisation of Cadell, with whom he subsequently worked very closely, heralded another new phase in Peploe's career. As Roger Billcliffe has explained:

> *Peploe set himself as a target the perfect still-life painting ... His temperament made him ideally suited to the task. His calm reasoning and thoughtful manner enabled him to make a careful analysis of the problems which face the still-life painter and he set about resolving them in a series of works which includes many of his most satisfying paintings.*[37]

The still lifes which Peploe painted during the period between approximately 1918 and 1923 are the works for which he is best known, partly because of the sheer number that he made and also because of their immediate and continuing commercial success. Peploe changed his technique, adopting an absorbent gesso ground and reducing the amount of medium in his paint. He pushed his use of colour to the extreme and obsessively arranged objects – such as blue-and-white Chinese porcelain vases, filled initially with tulips and then usually with roses; fans; books; fruit in a variety of dishes; fabric draped on tables, chairs and as a background; mirrors and jugs – to create finely balanced compositions. His niece Margery Porter recalled of her visits to his studio:

> *How well I recollect my Mother and myself climbing those steep stairs and arriving panting at the top to ring his bell in fear and trembling lest our climb had been in vain. But usually he would usher us in wearing a white painting coat and a crownless hat ... The studio was a large one, round which I would prowl entranced, after strict warnings not to disturb the still-life group which would almost inevitably be covering the table. My uncle would arrange and re-arrange these groups for perhaps three days before he was satisfied that the balance and construction were perfect, then he would paint them quite rapidly.*[38]

As Elizabeth Cumming explains, during this period Peploe explored the achievements of Cézanne, experimented alongside Cadell and created his own distinctive approach to the still life. As Honeyman recorded: 'Cadell's studio was about the only one S.J. ever visited. They often criticised each other's work, suggesting an improvement here and there, counselling eliminations of some passage or advising a fresh attempt.'[39]

However, by the mid-1920s Peploe had explored every possibility within this approach and his work evolved once more. Partly dictated by the seasons, flowers were often replaced by new props, including a statuette of the Venus de' Medici, a brown teapot, earthenware vases, loaves of bread and even lamb chops. The rusticity of Peploe's accessories was matched by a new low-toned palette, whilst his paint thickened and was applied with broader, more obvious and rigorous brushstrokes. The evolution from his sophisticated still lifes of pre-1910, through the experimental design-based still lifes of the pre-war period to the highly disciplined still lifes of the early 1920s was complete.

Peploe's landscape painting also developed apace during the 1920s. Whilst Cadell was fighting in the war, Peploe wrote to him:

When the War is over I shall go to the Hebrides, recover some virtues I have lost. There is something marvellous about those western seas. Oh, Iona. We must all go together.[40]

Cadell first visited Iona in 1912 and in 1920 he introduced Peploe to the island; they both returned most years thereafter [16]. In 1920 Peploe was nearly fifty years old, but Iona inspired a new direction in his work. Unlike Cadell, who painted a catholic range of subjects all over the tiny island, during the next fifteen years Peploe concentrated on analysing the rocks and sands of the north end and views from it, especially of Ben More on nearby Mull. Cadell teased him about this fixation, saying that he would do 'anything to escape the horrors of Ben More, Loch na Keal and Burgh!'[41] In contrast to Cadell however, whose depictions of Iona are invariably bathed in glorious sunshine, Peploe was interested in the challenge of conveying the wind, rain and even storms of the ever-changing weather conditions experienced on the island; in this his work has been compared to that of William McTaggart (1835–1910).[42] In 1923 Peploe wrote to the painter William Macdonald (1883–1960):

We had miserable weather in Iona this year – worst in living memory – gales and rain the whole time. I got very little done. But that kind of weather suits Iona: the rocks and distant shores seen through falling rain, veil behind veil, take on an elusive quality, and when the light shines through one has visions of rare beauty.[43]

Peploe initially lodged with the MacInneses at Cùlbhuirg, the principal farm in the west of Iona. Later, he and his family rented Lovedale in the village street.[44] Despite his reputation for introversion, islanders remember him allowing young boys to carry his palette and to watch him at work.[45] Once, when questioned by a visitor from Edinburgh as to why he was friendly with the locals, Peploe retorted: 'My dearest wife is a native of these islands and if ever I had the great misfortune to lose her, it would certainly be to these islands where I would look for her replacement!'[46]

France and other areas of Scotland continued to provide inspiration for Peploe's landscape painting, to which he was committed until the end of his life. Having first worked in Cassis in 1913 with Fergusson [44], Peploe returned there in 1924 with Cadell [63] and was drawn back again in 1928 and 1930 to paint the Mediterranean climate which was so different from that of the Western Isles. In 1928 Peploe also worked in Antibes, alongside George Leslie Hunter.

During the 1920s and early 1930s, Peploe found inspiration in the Scottish landscape of Dumfries and Galloway, Perthshire and Inverness-shire. He returned to Kirkcudbright and painted in Douglas Hall and New Abbey as well. Calvine and St Fillans drew him northwards, whilst the final and most northerly places that he painted were Boat of Garten and Rothiemurchus, where he painted his last picture.[47] Peploe's interest in trees as subject matter became increasingly pronounced, as discussed by Elizabeth Cumming.

After the war, Peploe's professional reputation grew steadily in Scotland, England and abroad. He worked hard and exhibited regularly. Honeyman recalled:

[17] S.J. Peploe with students, Edinburgh College of Art, 1934

He took little or no part in either the initiation or the promotion of any of the exhibitions of his work ... Whenever a sufficient number of paintings were completed, Peploe would arrange them round the walls of his studio. Reid, MacDonald or George Proudfoot [who joined The Scottish Gallery in 1908] *... would call, select the canvases they wished to buy, assemble them in a bunch and then depart. The following day a cheque for the total would be dispatched, Peploe would indicate approval and that was that.*[48]

From 1921 The Scottish Gallery and La Société des Beaux-Arts agreed to operate a half-share system with Peploe, splitting all sales of his work fifty–fifty; he thus gained a high profile in Edinburgh and Glasgow.[49] Following the formation of Alex Reid & Lefèvre in 1926, Peploe also had several solo exhibitions in London. When Reid & Lefèvre closed in Glasgow in 1932, Peploe was taken on by Pearson & Westergaard, who held a solo exhibition of his work in 1934. Throughout, Peploe continued to send to the RGI and RSA, as well as sending to the SSA in 1930, for the first time since 1919 and for what proved to be the last time.

Moreover, Peploe's work was included in several important group exhibitions, organised by McNeill Reid and Duncan MacDonald, in London, Paris and New York between 1923 and 1932. Peploe exhibited alongside Cadell and Hunter at the Leicester Galleries in London in 1923 and again in 1925, with the addition of Fergusson. In 1924, their work was shown at the Galerie Barbazanges in Paris, and in 1931, joined by George Telfer Bear (1876–1973) and Robert Ossory Dunlop (1894–1973), they were shown at the Galeries Georges Petit. In 1932 the work of the quartet was shown at Barbizon House in London, accompanied by Bear and William Gillies (1898–1973). In 1928, Peploe had a solo exhibition at the C.W. Kraushaar Art Galleries in New York.

The contrast between Peploe's reception in France and in America showed how the significance of his new work was recognised in some quarters, but not in others. In France, Peploe received the highest possible honour when the French state acquired a work from both the 1924 and 1931 exhibitions.[50] Peploe wrote to Fergusson: 'I think we may fairly congratulate ourselves on the event. If I had been told in 1911, when we were in Paris, that I should have a picture in the Luxembourg [the museum of contemporary art] by then, would I have believed it possible?'[51] On the other hand, in New York, where Peploe was unknown and his prices were considered high, only two works were sold and a planned tour to Chicago came to nothing. *American Art News* damned the Kraushaar exhibition with faint praise by describing the works as 'sincere and workmanlike performances' whilst Duncan MacDonald lamented to John Kraushaar:

I regret ... that the Peploe exhibition was not a greater success and as he is so good an artist I am surprised that the New Yorkers did not rise better to your enterprising exhibition. It was very courageous as well as kind of you to give this man a show and I certainly think his work was worth it. But I would have liked that you should have had more profit out of it.[52]

However, official recognition for Peploe's achievements grew during the 1920s: the Tate acquired *Tulips* of 1923 for the British national collection in 1927, the year in which he was elected a member of the RSA. His appointment was announced in the *Glasgow Herald,* which described him as 'an artist of the new movement, Mr Peploe is outstanding in Scotland, and his work has received recognition in London and abroad as well as at home'.[53] Peploe greeted this with his customary wariness, preferring to concentrate on painting and limiting his resultant administrative and teaching responsibilities as much as he could. Peploe presented *Boy Reading* [31] to the RSA as his diploma work.

The last years of Peploe's life were marred by ill health. Despite this and surprisingly given his reluctance to participate in the art world, he was persuaded by Hubert Wellington, Principal of Edinburgh College of Art, to accept a position on the college's teaching staff in 1933 [17]. Guy Peploe argues that he did so 'because of his sense of owing something to his profession and of his wishing to give something back, without didacticism; sharing, rather, a lifetime's accumulation of knowledge and wisdom without restraint'.[54] Peploe's first-hand knowledge of the historic developments in Paris before the war combined with his outstanding professional achievements gave him unique academic and practical expertise. Wellington declared: 'His influence was admirable, his standards high, his criticism acute, often unexpected, not to be anticipated by any formula, and there was a general rise in the keenness and effort of his class.'[55] Unfortunately, by the following session, Peploe's declining health meant that William Gillies had to take over his duties.

Peploe's last solo exhibition was held at Reid & Lefèvre in London in March 1934. That year it was hoped that a final new studio, at 65 Castle Street, would provide inspiration as previous changes had done. As Cursiter recorded: 'a light scheme of colour was selected again, a dark floor and strong notes of colour in draperies and accessories … but in this studio he painted only two pictures'.[56] He died aged sixty-four, on 11 October 1935 at a nursing home at 35 Drumsheugh Gardens, following an operation. The causes of death were given as 'exophthalmic goitre' (hyperthyroidism) and 'auricular fibrillation' (disrupted heart rhythm). A memorial service was held on 14 October at the Church of St John the Evangelist and Peploe was buried in the family grave in the Dean Cemetery, alongside his mother, father, nanny and brother William.[57] His estate was valued at £11,492:3:1, which was left in its entirety to Margaret.[58] Margaret survived him by twenty-three years. She never remarried and she remained at 13 India Street until her death on 23 October 1958; she too was buried in the Peploe family grave.

Peploe's death was widely reported and he was given obituaries in *The Scotsman*, *Glasgow Herald* and *The Times*, amongst other newspapers. David Foggie described Peploe as 'one of the most interesting and inspiring of Scottish painters … one of the few whose works were highly esteemed not only in Scotland, but in England and abroad'.[59] Memorial displays were held at the RSA and RGI in 1936. Substantial memorial exhibitions were held at The Scottish Gallery that year and at the McLellan Galleries, Glasgow in 1937.

But what of Peploe the man? He had a particularly happy marriage and family life [88]. Margaret Peploe recalled:

Sam was extremely modest about himself and his work … [it] pleased and surprised him to find people liked him … he was so unaware of himself, of his own many attractive qualities. Sensitive and shy, never physically very strong himself, he had a great admiration for the strong clean healthy type of man like J.D. Fergusson … Sam loved his own home and I like to remember how contented and happy we were.[60]

Of his physical appearance, Cursiter recounted:

He was tall and slim, he had a well-modelled head with a firmly marked nose, a rounded chin, a sensitive mouth, his moustache was close clipped, he wore eyeglasses, his hair was neatly trimmed – he was wholly unlike the traditional artist … He wore the conventional clothes of a man of affairs; an unobtrusive check on his grey or brownish suiting … even in his old suits, splashed with paint as they sometimes were when sketching in Iona, he looked well dressed.[61]

He was steeped in historical and contemporary literature and counted George Moore, Henry James, George Meredith, Oscar Wilde, Arthur Symons, Walter Pater and Thomas Hardy amongst his favourite authors. His sense of humour, though generally demonstrated in private, showed quick wits. One day, the Peploes were viewing a suite stuffed with horsehair at the Edinburgh furniture makers and designers Whytock & Reid, as a potential purchase for their drawing room. On being told its price, Peploe retorted: 'You must be stuffing them with Derby winners.'[62]

He was also musically talented, as Fergusson recorded:

We were very much interested in the latest music and its relation to modern painting. S.J. played the piano most sympathetically. I had in my studio one of the first pianos signed by Dettmer. When he came, Peploe always played it with complete understanding of the difference between it and an iron-framed grand. S.J. at the old piano is one of my happiest memories.[63]

Margaret Peploe summed up her feelings in 1939: 'He was a wonderful man my beloved Sam with his great beautiful mind and his innate integrity and so modest that he was utterly unaware of it all … something infinitely fine and beautiful passed with him.'[64] His brother-in-law, Dr Frederick Porter, concluded: 'A great artist, yes – and a great man.'[65]

[18]

Gipsy, late 1890s

Oil on canvas, 36.5 × 36
Private collection

[19]

A Windy Day at Barra, 1903

Oil on panel, 24.1 × 29.2
The Ellis Campbell Collection

[20]

North Berwick Sands, *c*.1896

Oil on canvas, 38 × 31 · Fife Council Museums: Kirkcaldy Museum & Art Gallery,
purchased as part of the J.W. Blyth Collection with the assistance of the Local Museums Purchase Fund
and the Art Fund (Eugene Cremetti Fund), 1964

[21]

The Lobster, *c*.1901

Oil on canvas, 41 × 51
Private collection, courtesy The Scottish Gallery, Edinburgh

[22]

The Coffee Pot, *c*.1905

Oil on canvas, 62.8 × 83.8
Private collection, courtesy Susannah Pollen Ltd

[23]

Still Life, Painter's Materials, late 1890s

Oil on canvas, 41.1 × 51.1
Aberdeen Art Gallery & Museums Collections,
The Hyslop Collection Bequest, 1993

[24]

*Self-portrait, c.*1900

Oil on canvas, 50.8 × 40.6
Scottish National Portrait Gallery, Edinburgh,
presented by John Thorburn, 1947

[25]

Mrs Peploe, *c.*1907

Oil on canvas, 61.4 × 51.3
Aberdeen Art Gallery & Museums Collections,
The Hyslop Collection Bequest, 1993

[26]

Girl in White, *c.*1907

Oil on canvas, 84.5 × 61.5
Private collection

[27]

Still Life, *c*.1912

Oil on canvas, 55 × 46
Scottish National Gallery of Modern Art, Edinburgh,
presented by A.J. McNeill Reid, 1946

[28]

Tulips and Fruit, *c*.1912

Oil on canvas, 46 × 56
Private collection, courtesy Christie's

[29]

*Kirkcudbright, c.*1918

Oil on canvas, 52 × 63
Dumfries and Galloway Council (Kirkcudbright Common Good Fund Collection,
The Stewartry Museum, Kirkcudbright), purchased with assistance from the National Fund for Acquisitions,
National Museums of Scotland, 1992

[30]

Flowers and Fruit (*Japanese Background*), *c.*1915

Oil on canvas, 46 × 30

Fife Council Museums: Kirkcaldy Museum & Art Gallery,

purchased as part of the J.W. Blyth Collection with the assistance of the Local Museums Purchase Fund and the

Art Fund (Eugene Cremetti Fund), 1964

[31]

Boy Reading, early 1920s

Oil on canvas, 76.2 × 63.5
Royal Scottish Academy Diploma Collection
(deposited 1927)

3 · PEPLOE IN FRANCE: 'A SUITABLE MILIEU'

FRANCES FOWLE

PEPLOE HAD A LIFELONG LOVE of France. He trained there, worked and holidayed there on numerous occasions, learned the language and made Paris his home for nearly two years. As a result of his exposure to Impressionism, Fauvism and Cézanne's proto-Cubism he was constantly reassessing his work and British critics frequently commented on the French influence on his developing style. We can tell from Peploe's letters that in his own mind he associated France and the French with creativity, openness and flair – the antithesis of his own Presbyterian shyness and inhibition. In 1907 he wrote to his future wife, Margaret Mackay, 'I do like the French people; they always remind me of the Gaelic – so frank and open … They so enjoy life, largely in an animal way.'[1] Peploe firmly believed that France somehow unlocked the creative, expressive side of his temperament. Above all, he adored Paris, and one of the highlights of his career was in 1924 when one of his paintings was acquired by the French state for the Musée du Luxembourg.[2]

It was J.D. Fergusson who invited Peploe to live in Paris, and his role in encouraging his friend's artistic development was crucial. On the other hand, Fergusson's influence has often been emphasised to the extent of eclipsing Peploe's individuality. This is due not only to Fergusson's overpowering personality in comparison to his more reserved companion, but also to the fact that much of what we know about Peploe's Paris period is based on Fergusson's selective and rather truncated memory. Despite this, contemporary accounts reveal that from the outset Peploe was Fergusson's equal and that, more often than not, his work was held in greater esteem. This essay aims to redress the balance through a thorough re-examination of Peploe's assimilation of French art in the period leading up to the First World War.

Like many British artists at the end of the nineteenth century, Peploe spent some time as an art student in Paris. In November 1891 he enrolled at the popular Académie Julian in the rue du Dragon, just off the boulevard Saint-Germain, where he was taught by the academic artist William Bouguereau.[3] He remained in Paris for at least six months, lodging in the avenue Victoria, in the centre of the city. In January 1894 he was back in Paris with his Aberdonian friend Robert Brough, with whom he shared rooms at 16 rue de Grenelle, only a short walk from Julian's. This time the two men found themselves under the tutelage of Jean-Paul Laurens (1838–1921) and Benjamin Constant (1845–1902), both renowned Orientalists, who, like Bouguereau, visited the studio on a bi-weekly basis.[4]

From the outset Peploe found Paris a stimulating city: 'There you have the camaraderie,' he wrote, 'good talk – enthusiasm – you are among people who are in sympathy with you.'[5] At this date Peploe spoke no French and it is likely that he mixed mainly with other English-speaking artists. However, he was eager to see French art and he frequented the art galleries in the rue Laffitte, especially that of Paul Durand-Ruel, the dealer who first supported the Impressionists. Peploe took an intellectual interest in modern French painting, including among his extensive reading matter George Moore's *Modern Painting*, published in 1893.[6] Moore had strong opinions on the Impressionists. He admired Alfred Sisley (1839–1899) who, in his view, was 'in sympathy with … nature' and 'able to produce a superior though much less pretentious picture than the ordinary stereotyped Monet'.[7] Peploe equally sought to present nature in an honest and unpretentious manner, and Sisley was among the first French artists whose work he admired.

In the summer of 1894 Peploe made the pilgrimage

with Brough and others to Moret-sur-Loing, where Sisley still lived. They visited the famous church, just opposite the artist's house on the corner of the rue du Château (now the rue du Donjon) and the rue Montmartre. In a letter to his artist friend Joseph Alfred Terry (1872–1939), Peploe described 'the old church ... with its grey crumbling stones ... always different from the grey of a rainy morning to the warm flush of the evening sun – pure gold against the eastern sky',[8] from which one can infer that he had seen the four canvases by Sisley of the church at Moret that were included in the Salon du Champ-de-Mars that spring.[9]

Returning to Scotland at the end of the summer, Peploe would have had little or no opportunity to see impressionist art in Edinburgh. In Glasgow, on the other hand, the art dealer Alexander Reid stocked pictures by Edgar Degas (1834–1917), as well as one or two examples of Sisley, Claude Monet (1840–1926) and Camille Pissarro (1830–1903), which trickled into Scottish collections around this period and were occasionally exhibited at the RGI.[10] Nevertheless it was only in Paris that artists had the opportunity to see a representative selection of impressionist pictures.

Peploe returned to Paris in 1899, very probably with Fergusson,[11] who recalled that they visited the newly opened Salle Caillebotte at the Musée du Luxembourg with its extensive collection of impressionist paintings, and Durand-Ruel's gallery.[12] They may even have seen the exhibition of paintings by Monet, Pissarro, Sisley and Auguste Renoir (1841–1919) that was held that May at Durand-Ruel's, and which included thirty-four works by Sisley.[13]

Shortly thereafter Peploe's landscapes began to reveal the influence of Sisley and, to a lesser extent, Pissarro. This is most evident in the paintings he produced at Comrie. *A Street, Comrie* [47] of about 1900, for example, invites comparisons with some of the village scenes that Sisley painted in and around Louveciennes in the 1870s.[14] The choice of motif, light palette and loose brushwork are close to Sisley, but the atmospheric clarity is unmistakably Scottish. In another work of the period, *Spring, Comrie* [48] of about 1902 – a group of farm buildings viewed through a screen of trees – Peploe employs a decorative device used by Pissarro in works such as *Red Roofs, Corner of the Village, Winter Effect* (1877; Musée d'Orsay, Paris), which he would have seen in Paris. On the other hand, Peploe's palette is much cooler than Pissarro's and he has simplified colour and form.

In November 1903 Peploe exhibited some of the Comrie landscapes at The Scottish Gallery in Edinburgh, prompting mixed reviews from the press. James Caw commented that 'Some of his landscapes ... cleverly though they are placed upon the canvas, and vividly as they register flashing effects of light, are too reminiscent of such painters as Sisley and Pissarro to be quite convincing.'[15] At this date the art establishment in Scotland was still suspicious of French art, especially Impressionism, which was not only deemed to be too 'scientific' and even 'decadent' in its approach, but constituted an erosion of Scottish identity.[16] It was Peploe's challenge to assimilate French modernism while maintaining his individuality as an artist.

As Fergusson recalled, in the end it was not Sisley

[33] *Old Tom Morris*, late 1890s

Glasgow Life (Glasgow Museums) on behalf of Glasgow City Council, presented by the Trustees of the Hamilton Bequest, 1974

[34] Édouard Manet
Le Bon Bock, 1873

Philadelphia Museum of
Art, The Mr and Mrs Carroll
S. Tyson, Jr., Collection, 1963

[35] Édouard Manet
*Portrait of Victorine
Meurent, c.*1862

Museum of Fine Arts, Boston,
gift of C. Paine in memory of
his father, Robert Treat Paine
2nd, 46.846

[36] *The Green Blouse*,
early 1900s

Scottish National Gallery
of Modern Art, Edinburgh,
purchased 1941

and Pissarro, but 'Manet and Monet ... who really fixed our direction – in Peploe's case Manet especially'.[17] Manet's work was championed in Britain during the 1890s by George Moore and in May and June 1894, while Peploe was still in Paris, he was given an important retrospective of about fifty paintings at Durand-Ruel's gallery. We know that several Scottish artists, including Peploe's friend Charles Hodge Mackie (1862–1920), visited the exhibition, and it seems probable that Peploe did too.[18]

Peploe's understanding of Manet was reinforced by his reading of Moore. Moore admired Manet's 'instinctive' approach to painting, which he compared to that of Velázquez and Frans Hals.[19] In *Modern Painting* he devoted a long passage to Manet's masterpiece *Le Bon Bock* of 1873 [34], which he praised for 'its fine handling and direct expression', while admitting that 'it falls short of Hals'.[20] Peploe's portrait of *Old Tom Morris* [33] appears to be his response to Moore, since it combines the pose, palette and technique of *Le Bon Bock* with the bravura brushwork of the two Hals portraits that he could have seen in the National Gallery of Scotland in Edinburgh.[21]

By the turn of the century some of Manet's portraits could be seen in Scotland. The *Portrait of Madame Brunet* (*c.*1863; J. Paul Getty Museum, Los Angeles) was on show at the Society of Scottish Artists exhibition at the RSA in Edinburgh in 1900;[22] the following year the *Portrait of Victorine Meurent* of 1862 [35] was lent to the International Exhibition in Glasgow and was also on show at Reid's Gallery, which Peploe visited with Mackie.[23] In 1902 the critic D.S. MacColl discussed

the latter portrait in his influential book *Nineteenth-Century Art* as an example of Manet's 'new vision of the world'.[24] In particular he admired the way in which Victorine Meurent's head 'stood out not only by the blondness of its lighted parts but by that of the shadow as well: the whole head relieved as a pale object against the background'.[25] Peploe, it appears, absorbed this lesson and applied Manet's method in works such as *The Green Blouse* [36] of the early 1900s. He applied the same formula to his still lifes. The simplicity and general format of these works – typically an arrangement of objects on a white tablecloth, set against a dark background [22] – owe much to Manet's compositions of the 1860s,[26] and, to a lesser extent, his later oil sketches of cut flowers, which Peploe is less likely to have known.

In emulating Manet, Peploe was on safe ground, since by the turn of the century the artist's posthumous reputation was at its height. Moreover, even though he was then regarded as the leading 'Impressionist', he was essentially a studio painter, who exhibited at the Salon and only latterly employed the light palette and divided brushstrokes of his contemporaries. On the other hand, Peploe's technique at this period was extremely eclectic. In 1902 he was able to see Whistler's 1864 painting *Symphony in White No.2* (1864; Tate, London) at the RSA in Edinburgh, followed by the large Whistler retrospective of 1904. This stimulated his so-called 'white period'. He also admired, and to a certain extent emulated, the slick, *alla prima* (wet-on-wet) technique of John Singer Sargent (1856–1925), whom he probably met through Robert

Brough. These various influences may account for the fluid handling and creamy quality of paint which are features of Peploe's work up to around 1909.

From around 1904 Peploe and Fergusson began to travel annually to France, stopping off in Paris before continuing on to the Normandy coast. Fergusson's interest in Monet may have inspired them to work out of doors on the Côte d'Albâtre (Alabaster Coast) between Étretat – one of Monet's favourite sites – and Le Tréport. The fashion for seabathing and the development of the railway system had transformed what were once small fishing villages into popular seaside resorts. Both Étretat and Le Tréport boasted casinos, but Peploe and Fergusson remained on the beach, sketching the tourists and the view out to sea. In the summer of 1904 they were at Berneval, where Peploe produced a small group of rapidly painted panels, taking in the sweep of coast, the chalk cliffs and the holidaymakers on the beach. The two artists almost certainly based themselves in or close to Dieppe, which was popular with a number of artists, and where D.S. MacColl had a villa. As Fergusson recalled, 'We worked all day, drawing and painting everything. And we thoroughly enjoyed the food and wine.'[27]

Moving farther along the coast, the two friends stayed at Étaples and painted on the Côte d'Opale (Opal Coast) at Paris-Plage (now Le Touquet) and Berck [37]. Étaples was then a popular artists' colony, situated on the Canche estuary. The French artists Eugène Boudin (1824–1898) and Henri Le Sidaner

(1862–1939) were among the earliest to work there. The town also attracted a number of American, Irish and British painters, among them the English Impressionist Philip Wilson Steer (1860–1942), who worked there in 1887, and William Lee Hankey (1869–1952), who built a house in Paris-Plage and had a studio in Étaples. According to one account, an added attraction for artists was the relatively low cost of accommodation:

> The usual plan is to live in rooms or studios and eat at the Hôtel des Voyageurs or Hôtel Joos – unpretentious hostelries with fairly good meals, served in an atmosphere of friendliness and stimulating talk … Artists pay about twenty-five or thirty francs a week for board and rooms, and studios are cheap.[28]

A large group of small plein-air oil sketches has survived from these trips. The earlier sketches, such as *Paris-Plage* [49] and *Wind* (*c*.1905; Kirkcaldy Museum & Art Gallery) are reminiscent in format, handling and tonality of Boudin's small panels of holidaymakers on the beaches at Trouville and Deauville, which Peploe could have seen at Alexander Reid's gallery. However the creamy texture of paint is more distinctly Peploe's.

At this date Fergusson and Peploe were working side by side and it is often difficult to tell their work apart. By about 1906 or 1907, however, Peploe's palette becomes much bolder, primary colours invade the canvas and the handling is more vigorous. In works such as *Bathers, Étaples* [38], even the subject is

[37] J.D. Fergusson (left) and S.J. Peploe, Paris-Plage, *c*.1905
Private collection, courtesy The Scottish Gallery, Edinburgh

[38] *Bathers, Étaples*, *c*.1906
Hunterian Art Gallery, University of Glasgow. Presented by Professor A. Macfie, 1973

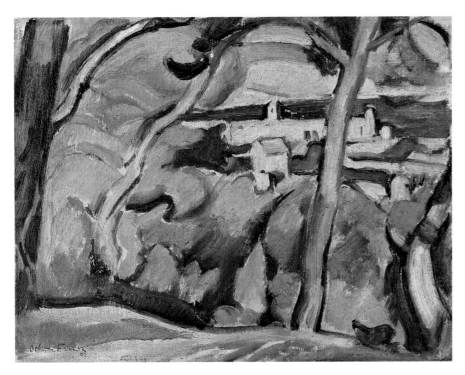

[39] Othon Friesz
La Ciotat, 1907

Amgueddfa Cymru – National Museum Wales

of Le Havrais artists such as Dufy and Friesz that, according to Vauxcelles, attracted most attention from the critics.[30] The Salon also included an important retrospective of work by Cézanne.

At this date, however, Peploe was more interested in Friesz, whom he later met through Fergusson. In 1907 Friesz exhibited five landscapes of La Ciotat on the Côte d'Azur, characterised by brilliant, non-naturalistic colour and rhythmic forms [39]. Peploe was also able to see his work that November at Eugène Druet's gallery in the rue du Faubourg-Saint-Honoré, and he had further exhibitions there in 1908 and 1910.[31] Friesz lived in Paris and had a studio at 55 boulevard du Montparnasse,[32] but from 1908 onwards he spent much of his time in his native Normandy and, like Derain, moved away from Fauvism as he came increasingly under the influence of Cézanne.

The other artist who caught Peploe's attention was Vincent van Gogh, who was given a major retrospective of fifty works at Druet's gallery in November 1909. It seems highly probable that Peploe visited the show since, from this date onwards, his work underwent a dramatic transformation. He began to experiment with Van Gogh's vivid but essentially naturalistic palette and expressive brushstrokes, and was also assimilating the main features of Fauvism.

It was in the summer of 1910 that the real turning point occurred in Peploe's work, evident in the paintings that he produced in Paris, at Veules-les-Roses [50] and above all at Royan. It was Fergusson who invited Peploe and his new wife to join him at Royan, a pretty town in the Charente-Maritime, on the west coast of France, south of La Rochelle. Situated at the mouth of the Gironde estuary, it enjoys a warm microclimate, which made it popular as a bathing resort from the mid-nineteenth century onwards.

Peploe recorded the most picturesque aspects of the resort, often setting up his easel close to the harbour. In *Boats at Royan* [41] he included the elegant tree-lined boulevard Thiers in the distance, but deliberately edited out the modern jetty, constructed in the late 1890s, and the paddle steamers, which were often moored alongside. In general he excluded the many tourists who gathered on the quayside or who strolled at a more leisurely pace along the town's boulevards and side streets. An exception is *Royan, Charente Inférieure* [51], a vigorously executed oil sketch, whose stabbing brushstrokes and vivid palette suggest an awareness of Van Gogh.

treated in an overtly modern way, suggesting an awareness of Matisse and the Fauves.

Through his friendships with artists such as Brough, who worked at Pont-Aven and Concarneau, and Mackie, a close friend of Paul Sérusier (1864–1927), Peploe was kept abreast of modern movements, including developments in colour theory.[29] He also corresponded with Fergusson and visited exhibitions and dealers in Paris while en route for the coast. A turning point came in 1905 when Henri Matisse (1869–1954), André Derain (1880–1954) and Maurice de Vlaminck (1876–1958) exhibited a group of vivid, crudely painted landscapes at the Salon d'Automne. The works that Matisse and Derain had produced at Collioure in the south of France took the Salon by storm, prompting the critic Louis Vauxcelles to label these artists '*fauves*' (wild beasts). Their raw expressive technique and fiery palette was soon adopted by painters such as Raoul Dufy (1877–1953), Othon Friesz (1879–1949), Georges Braque (1882–1963), Charles Camoin (1879–1965) and Albert Marquet (1875–1947), but was translated into a more rhythmic, toned-down version of Fauvism.

The movement was short-lived, however, and the last opportunity to see these artists was at the Salon des Indépendants and the Salon d'Automne of 1907. It seems probable that Peploe visited the Salon that year, if only to admire Fergusson's first submission. Matisse and Derain dominated the show, but it was the work

In other landscapes he is closer to Cézanne in his analysis of form and colour, but Peploe's work is always less architectonic than Fergusson's, his palette and handling closer to Friesz or even to the more muted colours of Marquet and Camoin than to the fiery Fauvism of Matisse, Derain and Vlaminck. Nevertheless the paintings that Peploe produced at Royan are distinctive for their vivid colour and bold technique. In works such as *Boats at Royan* [52] the paint is applied directly from the tube and areas of the primed canvas are allowed to show through, creating a sense of light and movement. The most striking feature of these landscapes is the use of colour to delineate form: warm reds and oranges to indicate sunlit areas and cool greens and blues to denote shadow. However, the palette lacks the boldness and discordant quality of Matisse's and Derain's paintings of Collioure. He also resists Fergusson's structural analysis and distillation of form in works such as *Royan* [42] of 1910.

Peploe's harmonising tones appealed to the critics and, despite some unfavourable reviews, he was generally regarded by the press as a better artist than Fergusson – one London critic remarking as early as 1908 that 'Mr Fergusson's studies are clever, of course, but this Franco-Scottish art has to be as good as Mr Peploe's before it satisfies either eye or mind.'[33] From the outset Peploe's art was always defined as 'Franco-Scottish', demonstrating his ability to assimilate French art while retaining his Scottish identity.

Returning to Paris at the end of the summer, Peploe rented an apartment at 278 boulevard Raspail, Montparnasse. As Fergusson recalled:

Peploe and I went everywhere together. I took him to see Picasso and he was very much impressed. We went to the Salon d'Automne where we met Bourdelle, Friesz, Pascin and others. He started to send to the Salon d'Automne.[34] *I was very happy, for I felt that at last he was in a suitable milieu, something more sympathetic than the RSA.*[35]

Peploe was welcomed by Fergusson's group of friends, which included a large contingent of American artists, among them Anne Estelle Rice (1877–1959), Jessica Dismorr (1885–1939), Bertha Case (1879–1970), the sculptor Jo Davidson (1883–1952) and Davidson's brother-in-law Louis de Kerstrat (1886–?). There was also a small circle of Scots, including the artists E.A. Taylor and Jessie M. King.[36]

Peploe relished the bohemian lifestyle and the intellectual stimulus that Paris provided. He sketched people at leisure in the Jardin du Luxembourg and accompanied Fergusson to the Café d'Harcourt and Boudet's restaurant where they once offered 'signed and dated portraits on the back of the bill' in lieu of payment.[37] He enjoyed the nightlife: the Concert Mayol music hall at 10 rue de l'Échiquier; the Théâtre de la Gaîté-Montparnasse; and the Cirque Médrano at 63 boulevard Rochechouart. The highlight, however, was Sergei Diaghilev's Ballets Russes, especially *Schéhérazade*, which was performed in Paris in 1910 with costumes and scenery designed by Léon Bakst.

Exposed to fauve painting, Peploe's technique became bolder and more experimental. A work such as *The Yellow Dress* [53], for all its sketch-like handling, shows the residual influence of Whistler in its narrow range of muted brown, blue and yellow tones, whereas the portrait of *Margaret Peploe* [54], painted around the same period, suggests an awareness of Matisse, especially in the application of green flesh tones to indicate the shadowed areas of Margaret's face. The use of complementary red outline in this portrait shows the impact of artists such as Rice, Dismorr and Marguerite

GATE OF THE LUXEMBOURG GARDENS. BY S. J. PEPLOE

[40] *Gate of the Luxembourg Gardens,* illustration from *Rhythm,* vol.1, no.1 (summer 1911)
Scottish National Gallery of Modern Art, Edinburgh

[41] *Boats at Royan*, 1910
Private collection

[42] J.D. Fergusson *Royan*, 1910
Hunterian Art Gallery, University of Glasgow

Thompson (1887–1968) who were developing a form of 'cloisonnist' painting, a practice acquired at the Académie de la Palette, where Fergusson taught. Their 'synthetist' style found its sources in stained glass, Japanese prints and (for Fergusson, at least) Celtic design. Émile Bernard (1868–1941), Louis Anquetin (1861–1932) and Paul Gauguin (1848–1903) had perfected this technique around 1888, painting in broad planes of pure colour surrounded by blue-black borders. Around 1910 Rice began to employ a red contour in works such as *La Toilette* (private collection), and Peploe applied this technique in several works, including his *Portait of a Girl, Red Bandeau* [55] of about 1912. Set against a blue background studded with red dots of paint, this frontal portrait also suggests the influence of Van Gogh, as well as Matisse.

Through Fergusson, Peploe became a regular artistic contributor to *Rhythm*, the modernist journal established by John Middleton Murry, an Oxford undergraduate.[38] Fergusson, as art editor, designed the cover for the first edition, published in the summer of 1911. It included illustrations by Picasso, Friesz, Rice, Dismorr and Peploe himself.[39] The leading article by Murry, entitled 'Art and Philosophy', gives a sense of the group's main aims, as well as Murry's awareness of the recent modernist debate initiated by the Bloomsbury Group artist and critic Roger Fry.[40] 'The role of the artist,' wrote Murry, was to attain 'pure form, refining and intensifying his vision till all that is unessential dissolves away ... He must return to the moment of pure perception to see the essential forms, the essential harmonies of line and colour, the essential music of the world.'[41] The basic tenet of the 'Rhythmists', as they became known, was that 'Modernism ... penetrates beneath the outward surface of the world, and disengages the rhythms that lie at the heart of things ... primitive harmonies of the world that is and lives.'[42] Murry's notion of 'rhythm' was inspired by Henri Bergson, especially his *Essai sur les Données Immédiates de la Conscience* of 1888, first published in English in 1910 (as *Time and Free Will*). Bergson identified 'rhythm' as the essential and unifying aspect of aesthetic experience.[43]

The writer Michael Sadleir also contributed a short article on Fauvism, which he defined as:

a frank reaction from the precious. It stands for strength and decision, alike of line, colour and feeling. It remedies the formlessness of Impressionism but keeps the brilliance.[44]

This was the approach favoured by the Rhythmists, including Peploe.

Peploe contributed to several editions of *Rhythm* and Murry's formalism is already evident in his two illustrations for the first edition. *Study* is a nocturnal scene of houses and rooftops, rhythmic and synthetist – reducing forms to their bare essentials. His second contribution was *Gate of the Luxembourg Gardens* [40], a black-and-white, simplified version of his brilliantly rhythmic oil sketches of the Jardin du Luxembourg, such as the panel now in The Fleming Collection [56]. Reviewing the first edition of *Rhythm*, the critic P.G. Konody remarked on the 'really excellent illustrations ... contributed by Miss Rice, Mr Peploe, Mr Fergusson and others; [and] some very bad ones by Picasso and Othon Friesz'.[45]

The synthetic style that is a feature of Peploe's illustrations for the first volume of *Rhythm* is also a feature of the works he produced that summer in Brittany. Peploe took the family to Santec, a village near Morlaix in Finistère, and painted with Fergusson on the Île de Bréhat. The most popular artists' colonies were at Pont-Aven – where Gauguin had lived and worked on and off between 1886 and 1891 – and Concarneau, and it was in this southern part of Brittany that most British artists, including Robert Brough, had congregated. The Île de Bréhat, by contrast, lies just off the north coast. The area had attracted French writers such as the Goncourt brothers and Pierre Loti (Julien Viaud), who visited nearby Paimpol. Peploe's Brittany canvases feature the modern holiday homes that had been built in the area, interspersed with more traditional thatched cottages [57]. The coloured contours and geometric simplification show that Peploe had fully aligned himself with the Cloisonnism of the *Rhythm* group. E.A. Taylor recalled that Peploe was 'tremendously taken up' with the Provençal Fauve Auguste Chabaud's (1882–1955) 'thick black lines and flat colours',[46] but Peploe's work is more nuanced, animated by the expressive brushwork of Van Gogh.

These decorative tendencies began to inform Peploe's still lifes and in 1911 he produced a series of startling images of tulips in brilliant primary colours. McOmish Dott was horrified with his latest work and urged him to revert to his previous manner, predicting that his new style would not appeal to the Edinburgh public. Peploe began to send work over to Alexander Reid's gallery in Glasgow, where he discovered a more receptive group of mercantile collectors, who under Reid's influence had already developed a taste for Impressionism. He hoped to discover a similarly more enlightened clientele in London, and in November 1911 he exhibited his recent still lifes in a joint show with Augustus John (1878–1961) and others at the Goupil Gallery. The reception, however, was mixed, one critic remarking that his tulips had 'certain unrestful decorative qualities which fail to charm'.[47]

London audiences were still wary of Modernism, as evidenced by their reception of Roger Fry's exhibition *Manet and the Post-Impressionists*, held at the Grafton Galleries from 8 November 1910 to 15 January 1911. The exhibition was intended to showcase the work of Gauguin, Cézanne and Van Gogh, which was shown alongside that of Manet, as the originator of Post-Impressionism, and a small selection of pictures by Matisse, Derain, Vlaminck, Friesz, Picasso, Georges Seurat (1859–1891), Paul Signac (1863–1935) and others.

Peploe was in Paris at the time of Fry's first exhibition and may not have seen the show, but he is certain to have heard the extreme press reaction. Robert Ross, writing in the *Morning Post*, commented that 'the emotions of these painters (one of whom, Van Gogh, was a lunatic) are of no interest except to the student of pathology and the specialist in abnormality'.[48] Desmond McCarthy, who assisted Fry in putting the exhibition

[43] W. Fox Pitt
The Stafford Gallery, 1912
Tate, London

together, reported that '[t]he ordinary visitor collapsed with laughter at the sight of the Cézannes; one elderly man ... went into such convulsions of laughter on catching sight of Madame Cézanne that his companion had to take him out and walk him up and down in the fresh air.'[49]

Nevertheless, the exhibition inspired other supporters of the avant-garde – notably the critic and curator

[44] Anne Estelle Rice, S.J. Peploe, Willy Peploe and J.D. Fergusson, Cassis, 1913

Private collection, courtesy The Scottish Gallery, Edinburgh

Frank Rutter and Michael Sadler, Vice-Chancellor of the University of Leeds – to join the cause. Sadler was the father of Michael Sadleir (they spelled their names differently to avoid confusion) and an important early collector of Gauguin and Kandinsky. In November 1911 he was persuaded by Sadleir to lend several paintings from his own collection, including Gauguin's *Vision of the Sermon* (1888; Scottish National Gallery, Edinburgh) to an exhibition of works by Gauguin and Cézanne at John Nevill's Stafford Gallery in Duke Street, London.[50] The following year Peploe and Fergusson between them participated in three exhibitions at the Stafford Gallery [43], and there is no question that Sadleir was involved. In February Peploe was given a solo show, at which he sold eighteen pictures, and he held a further show of drawings in June.[51] His latest pictures were well received, the critic for the *Morning Post* commenting that his work 'would command an honourable place' in a collection of modern paintings.[52]

In 1910 Fry had acknowledged that Post-Impressionism had spread beyond France and that there were 'Americans, Englishmen and Scotchmen in Paris ... working and experimenting along the same lines'.[53] Despite this, and despite their success in London, he reportedly dismissed Peploe's and Fergusson's work as 'turgid and over-strained'[54] and failed to include either artist in his *Second Post-Impressionist Exhibition* at the Grafton Galleries in October 1912, favouring his own Bloomsburyites such as Vanessa Bell and Duncan Grant.

Anticipating this omission, it was presumably Sadleir who persuaded the Stafford Gallery to hold a concurrent show of work by the *Rhythm* group. Peploe and Fergusson exhibited alongside Jessica Dismorr, Anne Estelle Rice, Ethel Wright (1866–1939) and others. The critic P.G. Konody praised 'the work of a group of English and Scottish Post-Impressionists, headed by Mr Peploe and Mr Fergusson, who apply the new principles as passionately and fearlessly as their French fellow-workers';[55] C. Lewis Hind – author of *The Post-Impressionists*, published in 1911 – questioned the omission of the Rhythmists from the Grafton Galleries' exhibition and identified Peploe's landscapes and still lifes as 'the outstanding feature of the show'.[56] Other critics identified Peploe as the 'leader' or 'master' of the group,[57] and Hind defined the Rhythmists' style as 'what may be called the Peploe–Fergusson branch of Post-Impressionism'.[58] With influential figures such as Hind and Rutter championing their cause, the Rhythmists had become an identifiable group, and Peploe was recognised as one of their leading representatives.

Therefore, when Peploe returned to Edinburgh in the spring or early summer of 1912,[59] he had established a reputation as one of the most important living artists in Britain. There is no question that he owed an enormous amount to Paris, Fergusson and the Rhythmists, but he had absorbed the lessons of Fauvism, while retaining his artistic identity.

Peploe probably retained his Paris studio until the early summer of 1913, by which date Braque and Picasso had astonished the world with their cubist still lifes and portraits, and even entered a second 'synthetic' phase. Peploe was only mildly interested in their analysis of space and form, producing a group of 'cubistic' still lifes around 1912. The faceted background and jagged outlines of *Still Life* [27] show an awareness of Cubism, but Peploe was not prepared to abandon realism.

He remained a Fauve at heart and in 1913 he made his first trip with Margaret and Willy to the Côte d'Azur.[60] Fergusson and Anne Estelle Rice had made the pilgrimage south a little earlier and had settled in Cassis, then a quiet fishing resort, around fifteen kilometres east of Marseilles [44]. They were following in the footsteps of fauve artists such as Camoin, who was there in 1905, and Derain, who worked in the area around Cassis in 1907, while Braque and Friesz were at nearby La Ciotat.

Lodged at the Hôtel Panorama, Peploe spent the summer working on a group of panels and canvases that show the continuing influence of the Rhythmist group. This is especially evident in *Square, Cassis* [45] with its jagged forms and synthetic Cloisonnism. Some of Peploe's views of the harbour, too, are dramatically cropped. *In Port, Cassis* [58] depicts men loading or unloading a boat, which is docked in the harbour, but the composition is highly abstracted, almost architectonic in its conception. Peploe evokes the heat of the day through the blanched colours, dark outlines and tiny hunched figures.

In March 1914 Peploe was given a solo exhibition at the Baillie Gallery in London. More than half of the thirty-nine paintings and nineteen drawings were of Cassis. The pictures were well received as the work of a 'Post-Impressionist' who had not 'succumbed' to abstraction. The critic for *The Studio* commented that 'Among English [sic] painters who have been affected by Post-Impressionism, Mr S.J. Peploe holds one of the first places,' praising him as

> *an artist whose head is stronger than the theories he has embraced … he gets the best out of them, gaining from what licence for freedom of line and abandonment to colour he may require, but preserving always evidence of contact with life as well* [as] *with theory, retaining vitality and the power to convince where so many under the same influence have entirely lost these.*[61]

In truth, of course, Peploe was already losing touch with the avant-garde. By 1914 Synthetic Cubism was at its height and Wyndham Lewis (1882–1957) was shocking the English press with his machine-like vorticist paintings. The critics preferred Peploe's more expressive naturalism, but it was becoming outmoded.

Peploe's love of France and French art did not diminish and he made three more trips to Cassis after the war. He stayed there in the spring of 1924,

lodging once again at the Hôtel Panorama.[62] In February 1928 he made another trip south, staying initially in Antibes, where Monet had painted exactly forty years earlier, before moving on to Cassis in mid-May.[63] His third and probably final trip to Cassis was early in 1930.[64] Trees were a common motif in these late works and, as Peploe's colour became more muted, the influence of Cézanne became more apparent. Perhaps staying in Provence in an area not far from L'Estaque, where Cézanne had also worked, was a reminder to Peploe of the esteem in which he had always held the French artist. A work such as *Landscape, Cassis, France* [59] of about 1924 invites comparison with Cézanne's *Big Trees* [46], inspired by the dense woodland on the Jas de Bouffan and in the area around Aix-en-Provence where Cézanne had been brought up. Peploe's approach is more decorative than Cézanne's, but he evokes the same sense of the tree as an integral, organic element in the Provençal landscape.

In conclusion, it is fair to say that Peploe's exposure to French art played a major role in the development of his style. From Manet he learned to apply paint instinctively and spontaneously; from Sisley he realised the joy of painting out of doors in front of the motif; from Friesz he learned to apply colour expressively without abandoning the internal 'rhythm' of his compositions; and from Cézanne he discovered a more

[45] *Square, Cassis*, 1913
Private collection

subtle analysis of form and colour. In Paris Peploe was able to immerse himself in the intellectual environment, absorbing the latest modernist debates, as well as developing the Cloisonnism of the Rhythmist group.

Peploe was consistently recognised, often ahead of Fergusson, as one of the leading post-impressionist artists in Britain. In 1914 the critic T.M. Wood estimated that the movement had 'taken upon itself a peculiarly national character in the hands of such artists as Mr J. Fergusson and Mr Peploe', defining 'purity of colour' as the essential quality of their work.[65] Certainly, Peploe's paintings have a distinct identity – whether this is a specifically Scottish identity is perhaps a matter for debate. He believed in using colour expressively, but always retained the internal balance of his paintings. Unlike some of the Bloomsbury artists, he was able to absorb the lessons of French Modernism without sacrificing his individuality. This, along with his technical brilliance and sense of colour harmony, marked him out consistently as the critically acclaimed leader of the Rhythmist group.

[46]   Paul Cézanne *The Big Trees*, *c*.1904

Scottish National Gallery, Edinburgh, presented by Mrs Anne F. Kessler, 1958; received after her death, 1983

[47]
A Street, Comrie, c.1900
Oil on canvas, 63.5 × 76.3
Private collection

[48]

Spring, Comrie, c.1902

Oil on canvas, 36 × 26 · Fife Council Museums: Kirkcaldy Museum & Art Gallery,
purchased as part of the J.W. Blyth Collection with the assistance of the Local Museums Purchase Fund
and the Art Fund (Eugene Cremetti Fund), 1964

[49]
Paris-Plage, *c*.1907
Oil on panel, 19 × 24
Private collection

[5 0]

*Veules-les-Roses, c.*1910

Oil on panel, 35.6 × 27
Scottish National Gallery of Modern Art, Edinburgh,
purchased 1965

[51]

Royan, Charente Inférieure, 1910

Oil on board, 24 × 33
Private collection,
courtesy Duncan R. Miller Fine Arts, London

[52]

Boats at Royan, 1910

Oil on board, 27 × 34.9
Scottish National Gallery of Modern Art, Edinburgh,
bequeathed by Dr R.A. Lillie, 1977

[53]
The Yellow Dress, *c*.1910

Oil on canvas, 61 × 50.8
The Ellis Campbell Collection

[54]
Margaret Peploe, *c*.1911

Oil on card, 35.3 × 27
Private collection, courtesy The Scottish Gallery, Edinburgh

[55]
Portrait of a Girl, Red Bandeau, *c*.1912

Oil on canvas, 46 × 38.5
Private collection, courtesy The Scottish Gallery, Edinburgh

[56]

*The Luxembourg Gardens, c.*1910

Oil on panel, 35.6 × 27.9
The Fleming-Wyfold Art Foundation,
purchased 1984

[57]

Île de Bréhat, 1911

Oil on panel, 32.5 × 40
Private collection

[58]

*In Port, Cassis, c.*1913

Oil on panel, 32.4 × 41.3
The Ellis Campbell Collection

[59]

*Landscape, Cassis, France, c.*1924

Oil on canvas, 63.5 × 53.5
Aberdeen Art Gallery & Museums Collections,
purchased 1993

4 · EXPLORING THE POETICS OF FORM: THE POST-WAR PAINTINGS OF S.J. PEPLOE

ELIZABETH CUMMING

IN THE IMMEDIATE pre-war years Peploe's art had been viewed in London as 'infected by the microbe of Matisse'.[1] The expressive energy of both brushwork and palette had been encouraged by both his residence in Paris and his ongoing visits to the south of France. His contribution to a mixed show at the Stafford Gallery had brought acclaim in London, with critics writing of his 'virile pictures ... exhilarating in colour and expressive in technique'.[2] Works such as the 'cubist' *Still Life* [27] are amongst the most ambitious paintings by any British artist in those years, sharply patterned using a broad brush thickly loaded with acid yellows, emerald greens and burnt orange, fiercely edged in blue. The bravura of these years would give way within a decade to a quieter, more empirical way of working.

The war had put a stop to Peploe's visits to France, and he was also increasingly bound to consider how best to support his family. His painting was not however in danger of becoming sober or dull: rather, his fascination with the ever-changing rigour of the still life continued and deepened. His goal was to concentrate hard on what lay in front of him, to match a means of expression to beauty of form – to succeed, as the critic Roger Fry had earlier written of Cézanne, in 'the power of finding in things themselves the actual material of poetry and the fullest gratification for the demands of the imagination'.[3]

The draw towards serious academic ambition coincided with Peploe's election as Associate member of the RSA in 1918. Such professional affirmation only further encouraged his ambition and his quest to explore the potential of that most academic of subjects, the still life. The formal approach of *Dish with Apples* (*The Ginger Jar*) [66] was underlined further by the very titles of paintings Peploe sent to the RSA in

1919 such as *Study – Volumes, Depth*. In these works, the design balance lies in beautifully lit and outlined forms and their shadows. Every object has its rightful place and the colour palette is chosen with absolute precision. The same approach was taken in a portrait of slightly later, *Girl in White* [65]. Here, Peploe's favourite oblique full-length positioning of the figure is offset by a still life – featuring the same ginger jar – to the right background and books to the left foreground. Colour and tonal values are controlled: whites, oranges, dark chair and table.

During the war relatively little of Peploe's work had been seen by the public, with only the standard couple of canvases (including a study of Jeannie Blyth) sent to the SSA, two per year to the RGI and drawings or still lifes to the RSA (this continued after the war). But with a family to support, dealerships became ever more vital to his success – although he never wished to become beholden to them, refusing, for example, to enter into a contract with Alexander Reid to supply a specified number of paintings per year. He had had his first one-man show in Glasgow with Reid in 1915 when over twenty Royan and Cassis subjects, plus some portrait and still-life studies, were sold.[4] It was the start of a positive dealer relationship, and also led to Reid introducing himself to Cadell in 1917.

Once settled in 1917 into his new airy top-floor Shandwick Place studio, Peploe began to experiment seriously with materials, applying an absorbent gesso ground to his canvases: apart from giving his colours vivacity, this would prevent reworking the following day and therefore enforced concentration. The end of war seems to have spurred him to embark on a new series of brightly coloured flower paintings, integrating his unapologetic new academicism with his confidence of colour. The result spelt modernity. Despite

[60] *Red and Pink Roses, Oranges and Fan*, c.1924
Oil on canvas, 61 × 51.1
Private collection, courtesy Christie's

his increasing fascination with Cézanne, Peploe was remaining loyal to the decorative values set out by Matisse.

Relatively few paintings from these immediate post-war years sold easily – an exhibition of rose paintings with Reid in November 1919 found the dealer buying seven for himself.[5] However, one client who did purchase these experimental paintings was Major Ion Harrison, whose family was in the Clydeside shipping business. He purchased both *Dish with Apples* and the lyrical *Tulips and Fruit* [68]. He bought not only Peploe but also works by Cadell and Hunter, and the collection would assist T.J. Honeyman to prepare his 1950 book, *Three Scottish Colourists*. Flowers in a blue and white vase, set on a table covered with perhaps a few books, a closed fan or a bowl of fruit against a bright blue cloth background was, in general terms, a typical subject right up to the end of his career but would be interpreted time and time again in a variety of ways. With cobalt blue a key colour partnered by acid yellows and oranges, his palette was carefully balanced by whites and reds. In *Tulips and Fruit* the forms are lightly edged, but not enclosed, with lines of a dry blue. Viewed together, such carefully orchestrated blasts of colour were extraordinary. As Harrison recalled thirty years later, 'I had never seen anything in art similar to these pictures, and I did not understand them. They really startled me for, to my eyes, they were so ultra-modern.'[6]

Despite setting his cap intellectually towards Cézanne, Peploe was thus continuing to apply French principles of decorative painting to his new-found formality. *Still Life with Tulips* [67] marks a new level in complexity. Set against a background of blue and black draped with lengths of green and white fabric, a chair painted red and draped in blue is placed behind a table on which are bowls, books, black ribbon and a vase of tulips. The flowers dance with those from two other vases located 'off canvas'. The rhythmist design of this canvas is brilliantly daring, developing elements from both *Tulips and Fruit* which are also seen in *Interior with Japanese Print* [69] of about 1919 where a loose assortment of objects are semi-scattered across the canvas.[7] Whereas the subject of this last painting might perhaps suggest the recent return of a couple from the theatre or opera, or simply an untidy studio, *Still Life with Tulips* has no such narrative pretensions but is rather a cleansed update of those bold, electric still lifes of 1912–13. These new paintings

also tell of Peploe's friendship with Cadell, with whom he shared compositional elements such as the red-painted chairs. Both artists were to explore colour arrangements within interior settings from the early to mid-1920s. *Interior with Japanese Print* rather than these first post-war still lifes shares the theatricality of Cadell's ultra-sophisticated Ainslie Place interiors of the early and mid-1920s. Such paintings as *Interior: The Red Chair* [61] demonstrate the influence of Peploe on him.

In August 1920 Peploe was persuaded to join Cadell on the island of Iona where he had first painted in 1912. It was the first of many visits, with Peploe exploring the entire island and particularly enjoying the character of the north end. The weather was not always good for painting. Peploe nonetheless joined Cadell on Iona most years, taking full advantage of the opportunity to look harder at the palette offered by nature. Here was an island where the colours and tonal values found in the rugged rocks could change from moment to moment according to the shifting west-coast light overhead. Iona, especially in good weather, is a place of deep beauty and, not least, steeped in Celtic history. Its abbey and other medieval buildings had been recently restored. More than any other place, Iona changed how Peploe worked, giving his art a new cohesion and depth. The relationship and unity of sea and shoreline held a special attraction for him. *Green Sea, Iona* [70] is an early example which has a particular balance of bejewelled colour and form across rock and waters to the hills of Mull beyond. The paint is applied vigorously with angled brushwork marking out the rocks, the turquoise sea beyond conveyed in horizontal sweeps of deep blues and greens.

The Iona paintings, evocative of its natural beauty, did well at The Scottish Gallery in the late winter of 1922 – his first show with his Edinburgh dealer since 1909 – and toured to Dundee with a further eight sales. Part of the paintings' success doubtless came from their combination of uplifting beauty and colour and a deep sense of Scottishness in these post-war years. They also fitted satisfyingly into a tradition since the mid-nineteenth century of celebrating the beauty of Scotland's landscape. These paintings of the early 1920s maintain an understated rhythm in a journey from the pre-war energised colour compositions to the classical simplicity which would peak just before the end of the decade. A sensitive portrait of his elder son Willy reading [31] is a good example of this quest

[61] F.C.B. Cadell
Interior: The Red Chair,
early 1920s
Private collection

[62] Peploe exhibition
at La Société des Beaux-
Arts, Glasgow, 1924
(from *Glasgow Bulletin*,
4 April 1924)
Tate, London

for reality. This strictly academic approach was driven by the market but was also a key part of his personal attitude to painting.

The Scottish Gallery and Alexander Reid recognised Peploe's art had entered a new phase, and now worked in partnership: from 1921 they agreed to part-share their purchases, splitting all sales of his work fifty–fifty. Thereafter both galleries held frequent one-man shows, some of which were substantial – in 1924 Reid displayed as many as thirty-five of Peploe's paintings, many of them Iona pictures which particularly attracted compliments [62].

As well as Iona paintings, the dealers showed what have since become 'classic' Peploe: his still-life studies of roses. Painted principally before 1924, these 'simple' vases of roses on a table, sometimes with a black ribbon, a fan or fruit to the side, become more complex towards the mid-1920s, much as Cadell's interiors and still lifes were to engage with an increase in textures, colour diversity and pattern. Flowers in season, roses following on from tulips, partner ceramic bowls or vases, set against a length of beautiful fabric (sometimes purchased from the Edinburgh furnishers Whytock & Reid), all so carefully selected, arranged and rearranged time and again before brush

was ever put to canvas. Stanley Cursiter recorded how, when teaching a course in advanced life painting at Edinburgh College of Art in 1933–4, Peploe would struggle to set up the model to benefit each student, and at times had simply to leave it to them to arrange.[8] *Still Life with Roses* [74] from about 1924 is one of the best: here Peploe combines a glorious symphony of colour with vigorous brushwork, with forms and shadows creating a network of line and slashes of quickly applied colour. He also revisits the neat device of introducing an off-canvas second vase to the right. In *Red and Pink Roses, Oranges and Fan* [60] and *Roses* [72] the various elements seem arranged to perfection, the delicate blue definition of each corresponding to the fragility of roses on the cusp of full bloom. All colours, strong and delicate, work in partnership, with oranges, blues and yellows supporting the purity of the roses' pale pink. These rose studies in a way may be almost endless permutations on a theme, yet no two are identical and each is treated with honesty and will.

Despite the appeal of Peploe's paintings to the Scottish collectors, his work was far from parochial. He remained in regular if not close touch with his fellow painters. In London, J.D. Fergusson was in contact with writers, musicians and art theorists; according to T.J. Honeyman, in 1922 with Peploe and Hunter he had hoped to invite Roger Fry north to Glasgow to give a series of lectures on modern art, but nothing came of it.[9] However, other links with London were being forged. At the start of 1923 Peploe was given top billing in a show with Cadell and Hunter organised by McNeill Reid at the city's Leicester Galleries. It achieved a huge amount of press coverage, with more than a dozen London and provincial English newspapers taking it up; but on the whole reviews were not kind. The *Yorkshire Observer* displayed the headline 'The bizarre in art: exhibition of paintings at the London Galleries', and the *Daily Telegraph* labelled the three 'the Scottish Extremists', considering that 'their modernity is characterised by a certain harshness of contour and garishness of colour that makes their work of a first introduction anything but pleasant to look upon'.[10] The *Morning Post*, under the snide headline 'Art and artists: three clever painters', was typical of other general reviews:

> Their outlook is towards decoration. Any emotion begotten of nature is stilled by compression within a formal design. Consequently they in the main limit their subject to what the French call nature-morte. Even when they forsake the beloved turnip, banana, rose, or bottle for a human being, the result is merely a mask, often quite charming, but lifeless. Look at the clever work of a triad now exhibiting at the Leicester Galleries, particularly at Mr. Peploe's flower pieces – his are the best in the triple collection ... .[11]

A legacy of the exhibition came from the review submitted by P.G. Konody, the art critic of the *Daily Mail* (and an accepted authority on French painting), who called his piece 'Scottish painters: the work of three colourists' – the first known application of the term 'colourist' to these artists.[12] He wrote: 'Mr Peploe, from his earliest beginnings, was one of the most daring and fascinating colourists of the British race. The change in his recent work is clearly due to the influence of the Frenchman Cézanne, who marks a new era in European art ... .'

Sales understandably remained much stronger north of the border. As an ARSA and latterly as a full Academician, Peploe continued to send to the RSA most years between 1923 and 1929, though less regularly to the RGI. Following a successful show with The Scottish Gallery, the Peploes returned to Cassis in the spring of 1924, with Cadell and his sister Jean joining them [63]. The weather was reasonable even if, as it turned out, the Hôtel Panorama left something to be desired. After Margaret and the boys returned to Edinburgh for school, Peploe wrote home, commenting that the hotel's pea soup was filling if indigestible.[13] In the evenings the men played billiards, a game of tactical skill, of eye-to-hand coordination and colour organisation – a game designed for painters if ever there was one. Peploe's Cassis oils from this spring employed subtly chosen local colour to give a real sense of heat and atmosphere. The sculptural forms of strong tree trunks were a feature which Peploe obviously relished, placing them right in the foreground, outlining them boldly and illuminating them with the dappled sunlight (see *Landscape, Cassis, France* [59]). He used fierce, broad brushstrokes in these Cassis paintings, working quickly to capture the effect of the strong sunlight, as seen in *The Aloe Tree* [79].

Cadell and Peploe's exhibition with Hunter and Fergusson as *Les Peintres de l'Écosse Moderne* was organised by Reid at the Galerie Barbazanges in Paris that summer. It marked a decided step forward in their reception both at home and abroad, with reviews in *Le Temps* and the *Gazette des Beaux-Arts*. The French government bought works by each Colourist with the exception of Cadell: Peploe's was a recent Iona oil.[14] The same summer Peploe and Cadell both had work included in the British Pavilion of the Venice Biennale, again arranged through Peploe's Scottish dealers.[15] Peploe fronted the line-up in the Leicester Galleries' own show of paintings by all four Colourists in January 1925. The painter Walter Sickert (1860–1942) in his preface to the latter exhibition's catalogue referred to Peploe's intellectual progress, a 'kind of rebirth', with his painting now carrying 'a certain kind of delicious skill to a pitch of virtuosity'. He opined that 'obviously beautiful as was Mr Peploe's earlier quality, his present one will establish itself as the more beautiful of the two'.[16] His art was now increasingly sought after, stimulated by critical approval but more by the strength and beauty of the work itself. It continued to be purchased principally by Scottish businessmen loyal to his dealers, including William Boyd in Dundee [64] as well as J.W. Blyth and Robert Wemyss Honeyman in Kirkcaldy. With income somewhat more reliable, the Peploes had been able to purchase their rented second-floor flat at 13 India Street in August

[63] Left to right standing: F.C.B. Cadell, Mrs Penny, Jean Cadell, Captain Penny; left to right seated: Margaret, Denis and S.J. Peploe
Photograph by Willy Peploe, Cassis, 1924
National Library of Scotland, Edinburgh

[64] William Boyd at home in West Ferry, Dundee, 1930s, with Peploe's *Girl in White* seen second from right
Private collection

1924. These were good years with fewer financial concerns: S.J. Peploe was in demand – in Scotland at least.

London galleries still tended to attract mixed reviews. *The Studio* wrote of his show at the new Reid & Lefèvre in late 1926 in mixed terms, referring to him as 'a painter of somewhat perverse originality ... his technical methods are a little too casual, but underlying them there is a foundation of sound knowledge of nature which saves his work from incoherence and gives it a satisfying measure of credibility'.[17] R.R. Tatlock in the *Daily Telegraph* wrote of a second show at this gallery in 1929 that he 'picks up his colours ... readymade from what he sees before him' while Cézanne arrived 'more indirectly at his statement'.[18] By contrast, the same show in *The Scotsman* hailed him as the 'Scottish Cézanne', with his work having 'a beauty of pattern, a power of handling and a purity of colour'.[19]

From the mid-1920s Peploe again revised his studio subject matter to run parallel to his study of landscape. *White Lilies* [73] and *The Ginger Jar* [76] of about 1926 are, like his early 1920s portraits and the later *Chops* [75], beautifully simple explorations of form – perhaps the closest he came to the absolute integrity of Cézanne, a reproduction of whose art he kept pinned up in his studio.[20] There was little obvious beauty in a piece of animal flesh but it was a traditional academic idea, and one which also demanded quick working. With a further loosening of brushwork came more muted, sometimes neutral, colours. By about 1930 Peploe was mastering extraordinary subtlety in such broadly painted canvases as *Roses and Fan* [77]. *Martagon Lilies* [78] is a sweet and tender evocation of the fragility of nature. By placing the lily to the far left, it almost seems caught off guard, like a snapshot. The composition looks relatively effortless, and, although modest, this is one of the most delicately beautiful paintings of his career.

The connection with Cézanne applied equally to portraits including his later oil of Willy [82], striking in its simplicity, and late landscapes where his deep fascination in the enduring monumentality of tree forms is obvious. In 1928 Peploe had returned to the south of France, this time painting at Antibes with Leslie Hunter, then at Cassis. Here the main dominant, permanent features of the landscape seem to have impressed themselves ever more on his consciousness [59]. *Trees, Antibes* [83] and *Blue Water, Antibes* [80] are also powerful, yet so simple, oils of trees, their trunks marked with vigour, their leaves and roots diffused into the landscape and sky. Back home, Peploe's landscapes also captured a deep sense of place, as in *Kirkcudbright* [81]. Visiting Boat of Garten he came across a forest glade dappled by sunlight, a good subject where he worked paint with vigour, applying it fast and thickly with a palette knife as well as brushes [86]. These later canvases are paintings of remarkably heightened sensations and each is unique. At the same time, he continued to exhibit still-life and Iona pieces, and they still drew attention. Writing of Peploe's modest contribution (a still life and an Iona canvas) to the 1929 RGI show, the London critic Frank Rutter rightly called Peploe the 'real leader of the forward movement in Scotland' and referred to his 'fresh, clean colour' and 'powers of simplification and synthetic design'.[21] The late work is passionate with a confident breadth of handling [84].

The 1930s confirmed the status of Peploe's position within contemporary art. Public art galleries began to take note: Manchester Art Gallery purchased *The Aloe Tree* [79] in 1930 from Reid & Lefèvre, following the Tate Gallery's purchase of *Tulips* (1923) from the dealer three years earlier, and Aberdeen Art Gallery would buy their 1928 oil of Cassis in 1933. He was again chosen for the Venice Biennale in 1930, and the following March McNeill Reid selected a display of his work with the other Colourists and also George Telfer Bear and R.O. Dunlop at Paris's Galerie Georges Petit.

Both of these painters – Telfer Bear in Edinburgh and Dunlop, founder of London's Emotionist Group in 1923 – were artists concerned with colour in their primarily decorative paintings, whether landscapes or figures in interiors. The Paris catalogue had a preface officially penned by the British Prime Minister, Ramsay MacDonald. Peploe's contribution of ten paintings covered the range of his production, from still lifes with roses or fruit and scenes of Iona or France to academic figurative studies. The French government purchased a second painting, a view of trees at Cassis. The exhibition transferred to London's Barbizon House. Peploe took a new studio in 1934 at 65 Castle Street on the corner with Queen Street, a short walk from home. He continued to paint in Scotland with his last visit to Iona in August 1935, a mere two months before his unexpected death.

That spring he had written of tulips as having 'so many colours: orange, pink, different pinks, a strange one – pure brick red – which is my favourite; so sensitive to warmth; the tulip with the strange hot smell which seems to stir deep memories, long-forgotten cities in a desert of sand, blazing sky, sun that is a torment; mauve ones, cool and insensitive'.[22] It seems that, despite failing health in his last two years, Peploe never lost his passion for colour and, above all, for his exploration through art of how it feels to be truly alive.

[65]
Girl in White, early 1920s

Oil on canvas, 71.1 × 51.1
Private collection, courtesy Christie's

[66]
Dish with Apples (*The Ginger Jar*), *c.*1918
Oil on canvas, 63.5 × 76.2
Private collection

[67]
Still Life with Tulips, *c.*1919
Oil on canvas, 74.9 × 61.5 · Private collection, courtesy Christie's

[68]

Tulips and Fruit, *c*.1919

Oil on canvas, 61 × 51
Private collection

[69]

Interior with Japanese Print, *c*.1919

Oil on canvas, 80 × 62.2
University of Hull Art Collection, purchased through the Ferens Fine Art Fund with the aid of a gift from
Mr J.W. Powell and grants from the Art Fund and the Victoria and Albert Museum, 1971

[7 0]

Green Sea, Iona, *c*.1920

Oil on canvas, 50.8 × 60.9
The Fleming-Wyfold Art Foundation,
purchased 1976

[71]
Pink Roses in a Japanese Vase, early 1920s

Oil on canvas, 50 × 40.5
Private collection

[72]

*Roses, c.*1924

Oil on canvas, 61 × 50.8
Private collection

[73]

White Lilies, mid-1920s

Oil on canvas, 61 × 51
Private collection, courtesy The Fine Art Society,
London and Edinburgh

[74]

*Still Life with Roses, c.*1924

Oil on canvas, 51 × 40.8 · Aberdeen Art Gallery & Museums Collections,
purchased with income from the Webster Bequest, 1942

[75]

*Chops, c.*1930

Oil on canvas, 45.3 × 40.5

Aberdeen Art Gallery & Museums Collections,

The Hyslop Collection Bequest, 1993

[76]

*The Ginger Jar, c.*1926

Oil on canvas, 45.8 × 55.9
Private collection, courtesy Christie's

[77]

Roses and Fan, *c*.1930

Oil on canvas, 45.7 × 40.6
Dundee Art Galleries and Museums (Dundee City Council),
purchased 1944

[78]

*Martagon Lilies, c.*1930

Oil on canvas, 44.5 × 39.5 · Ferens Art Gallery, Hull Museums, purchased 1981 by the Friends of the Ferens
with a 50% grant from the V&A Purchase Grant Fund in memory of Lesley Dunn,
Senior Keeper of the Ferens Art Gallery 1976–1981

[7 9]
*The Aloe Tree, c.*1924

Oil on canvas, 61 × 50.9
Manchester City Galleries, purchased 1929

[8 0]
Blue Water, Antibes, 1928

Oil on canvas, 63.5 × 63.5
Private collection

[81]

Kirkcudbright, late 1920s

Oil on canvas, 53.3 × 63.5
The Fleming-Wyfold Art Foundation, purchased 1978

[82]

Willy Peploe, *c*.1930

Oil on canvas, 77 × 61
Private collection, courtesy The Scottish Gallery,
Edinburgh

[83]

Trees, Antibes, 1928

Oil on canvas, 63.5 × 76.2
Private collection

[8 4]

*Landscape, South of France, c.*1928

Oil on canvas, 50.5 × 55.9
Scottish National Gallery of Modern Art, Edinburgh, purchased 1969

[85]

Iona, early 1930s

Oil on canvas, 45.5 × 56
Private collection

[86]
Boat of Garten, *c*.1929

Oil on canvas, 58.4 × 76.3
Private collection

5 · PEPLOE SINCE 1935

ELIZABETH CUMMING

'HIS VISION is not very subtle, and he is possessed by a perverse taste for the ugly or the bizarre in figure and landscape.'[1] National Gallery of Scotland director Sir James Caw had once dismissed Peploe, but thirty years on he revised his thoughts, writing of his 'decorative arrangement and splendid decision of handling' and, with perception, of his 'direct relationship to nature, intellectual rather than emotional perhaps, but pictorially satisfying ... the exceptional quality of Peploe's art will ensure him of a permanence and distinctive place among the more notable painters of his time'.[2]

Following Peploe's death the first article to review his career came from one of his dealers, T.J. Honeyman, who was then working for Reid & Lefèvre. Assessment would be a wrong term to use, as his article had been largely prepared weeks before the artist's death, perhaps to boost commercial sales at a time when Peploe's health was acknowledged to be in decline.[3] Illustrated principally by later landscapes and still lifes, the article neglected much of the early career and predicted – mistakenly, as it has turned out – that the phrase 'a great colourist' would be superseded by critics and historians by the wider term 'a great artist'.

Two posthumous exhibitions of Peploe's art were soon organised by his dealers. While the RSA set up a memorial display of eight paintings from across his career and the RGI showed five works, in April and May 1936 The Scottish Gallery presented a substantial memorial show of eighty-three works with a foreword by Caw to lend gravitas, if needed: Peploe had not sent much work to society exhibitions in the last few years. Caw now considered the early works as 'admirable in arrangement, and (the word is scarcely too high to describe the surety and élan of his painting) masterly in handling'.[4] More recently, Caw observed, 'balanced and self-contained design and stressed solidity of form' had marked out an individual way of working, making Peploe an artist independent of fashion. He referred to intelligence and character. With its many private loans returning to the gallery for the show it was a memorable display, probably one of the best mounted by a commercial gallery.

However, the most considered appraisal of Peploe's art came from his fellow artists. David Foggie, a recent colleague at Edinburgh College of Art, sent *The Scotsman* a detailed critique of the exhibition, with particular emphasis on the artist's daring change of direction in the 1920s from an easy virtuoso, painterly style and traditional colour harmonies to 'severely intellectualised arrangements in dry pigments'.[5] For Foggie the artist, this was a brave step and marked out Peploe's honesty and greatness in maturity: no pandering to fashion as he strove to place acid colours together as never before, cold whites, grey purples, vermillion and yellows. Every painting was an experiment, with many a failure to be discarded. Foggie got it right, and his article as well as the exhibition broke new ground in assessing the artist. J.W. Blyth, who had lent no fewer than fourteen pictures back to The Scottish Gallery, wrote to *The Scotsman* to express his pleasure at Foggie's review, adding that after many years of 'joyous' living with Peploe's art he found them 'both tender and sympathetic'.[6]

Glasgow also paid homage. The following February Reid & Lefèvre's tribute was organised in association with Pearson & Westergaard, Peploe's later west Scotland dealer, at Glasgow's McLellan Galleries: well over a hundred paintings were on display, making it the largest ever show of the artist. The catalogue was prefaced by a tribute from his friend E.A. Taylor. The same year the RGI annual exhibition included five

[87] Detail from *Martagon Lilies*, c.1930 [78]

paintings – a girl in white, an Iona piece and three still lifes. Then, just before the Second World War, Peploe's painting began to be seen in context – with Hunter and Cadell, also by now deceased, at Reid & Lefèvre in London and in a wider company at the Royal Academy as part of its *Scottish Art* exhibition of 1939, a transfer of art shown at Glasgow's Empire Exhibition the year before. Reid & Lefèvre's catalogue had as fine an introduction as The Scottish Gallery's three years earlier, this time from the pen of Douglas Percy Bliss, artist and director of the Glasgow School of Art. Bliss wrote of these painters as true modernists, eschewing fashionable subject matter in favour of expression. He equated them with sonneteers, reworking a subject many times for new challenges, and in the case of Peploe referred in turn to critic William Hazlitt's essay on the 'conscious keeping' and 'internal design' of Nicolas Poussin (1594–1665), the artist whose classical clarity of form and intellectual vision had so inspired Cézanne. In his tribute Bliss was setting Peploe in their company.

Stanley Cursiter, Caw's successor as director of the National Gallery on the Mound, was active in showing Scottish art and design during the war.[7] In 1941 he presented concurrent exhibitions of Peploe's and McTaggart's paintings, comparing two artists concerned at different periods with the identity of the national landscape. Sixty-three paintings were shown. Like Foggie, Cursiter the artist understood Peploe. His exhibition was accompanied by a perceptive essay which outlined his career but also significantly provided a critique of Peploe's quest for 'the common ground on which form and colour meet'. His close analysis of the painter's struggles to resolve colour by building up and discarding textures brought alive the art, and still today remains a core text. It would form the basis of Cursiter's biography, to be written in the next few years with the assistance of Margaret Peploe who requested long-standing friends, including J.D. Fergusson and E.A. Taylor, to supply information and memories where possible.

The biography, eventually published in 1947, is sympathetic. Well illustrated for these years of austerity, it was written, like his exhibition introduction, for both the artist and the layman, and aimed to explore the influences on Peploe at various periods. Publicity for the book referred to the artist's international reputation. Only the biography by Peploe's grandson Guy has followed, first published to coincide with the major *Scottish Colourists 1900–1930*[8] show of 2000 and recently revised, but this has a quite distinct character in its liberal use of personal letters to and from friends and family.[9] Fergusson's 'Memories of Peploe' essay was initially written in 1945 for Cursiter's book and was published posthumously in its own right in the *Scottish Art Review*.[10]

T.J. Honeyman depended more than Cursiter on Fergusson's recollections when he came to write his account of *Three Scottish Colourists* in 1950. From this date onwards 'Peploe studies' shifted naturally towards historical appreciation and analysis. Honeyman, now no longer trade but ranked as 'art establishment' as director of Glasgow Art Gallery (Kelvingrove), had contributed an introduction to the catalogue for the group show of *Paintings by Four Scottish Colourists* at T. & R. Annan in the city in 1948. The Edinburgh Festival in 1949 provided an international platform for showing Peploe with Cadell and Hunter, followed in 1953 by Peploe's younger son Denis's travelling exhibition of nearly sixty paintings for the Scottish Committee of the Arts Council of Great Britain: his catalogue essay presents his father as a romantic painter, a man of outstanding devotion to his art whose reputation was growing year on year.

However, much of the 1950s and 1960s saw a dip in the visibility of Peploe's art. Nearly two decades passed before the (now) Scottish Arts Council presented *Three Scottish Colourists* in eight galleries across Scotland in 1970. By now critical appraisal of art had been expanded to include the new professionals, the art historians. Critical writing always goes in fashions, and so, with interest from the late 1960s generally focusing on the turn of the nineteenth century – from Whistler and the Impressionists to the Arts and Crafts movement – it was not surprising that historians for the next two decades concentrated on Peploe's pre-war paintings. For *Three Scottish Colourists*, Bill Hardie referred to Cursiter's and Fergusson's published memories in his introduction, and positioned the painters within the Franco-Scottish tradition. Cézanne and Matisse were acknowledged as the painters' inspiration, with the Scottish 'logic' of colourist work determined by the material. In the mid-1980s the Francophile nature of early-career Peploe was touched on in my own contextual exhibition on J.D. Fergusson, also prepared for the Scottish Arts Council in 1985.[11] That summer, Guy Peploe, some thirty-two years after his father, curated a definitive show of over 200 examples of his grandfather's art, this time at the Scottish National Gallery of Modern Art. Ever since, Peploe work has appeared in many surveys of Scottish and also British art, as well as showing with major dealers and auction houses. Since the late 1980s the latter, through their dedicated Scottish Colourists sales, have steadily led the resurgence of interest in the Colourists. Despite exclusion from some major survey shows of British art, including that presented by the Royal Academy in 1987, both Fergusson and Peploe appear on the syllabus of Scottish art education, and the influence of Peploe's short period of teaching at Edinburgh College of Art has been lasting.

In our century the later paintings have come properly into their own and a balanced view of Peploe's career is possible, as witnessed in this exhibition. Now, perhaps, Roger Fry's 1910 critique of Cézanne might be seen as having almost equal application to Peploe: '[s]ince Chardin no one has treated the casual things of daily life with such reverent and penetrating imagination'.[12] Peploe continues to attract interest from the public, and collectors remain ever keen to buy, with auction prices edging close towards a million pounds. Peploe's art is still being purchased, as funds allow, for public collections. Yet any artist is seen quite differently not only at various points in his or her career but within and beyond a lifetime – and there is and will always be room for another interpretation.

[88] S.J. Peploe with Margaret, on Princes Street, Edinburgh, *c*.1930
Private collection, courtesy The Scottish Gallery, Edinburgh

CHRONOLOGY

1871
Samuel John Peploe born on 27 January at 39 Manor Place, Edinburgh.

1874
Birth of sister Annie Margaret Peploe and death of mother Annie Hickock Peploe.

Birth of John Duncan Fergusson, 7 Crown Street, Leith.

1877
Birth of George Leslie Hunter, 7 Tower Street, Rothesay, Isle of Bute.

1883
Birth of Francis Campbell Boileau Cadell, 4 Buckingham Terrace, Edinburgh.

1884
Death of father Robert Luff Peploe. Peploe, his elder brother William Watson Peploe and their sister Annie are brought up by their nanny Mary Sanderson, under the guardianship of eight trustees and their half-brother James Reid Peploe. Peploe attends Edinburgh Collegiate School and is apprenticed to the solicitors Scott & Glover, amongst other attempts at establishing a career.

1889
Alexander Reid opens his gallery, La Société des Beaux-Arts, in Glasgow.

1891
Peploe enrols at the Académie Julian, Paris, to where he returns for periods until 1894.

1892
Peploe enrols in the Royal Scottish Academy Life School which he attends until 1896.

1894
First of several painting trips to the Hebridean island of Barra, where meets Margaret Mackay, his future wife.

1895 *or* **1896**
Study trip to Holland.

1896
First of several painting trips to North Berwick.

By this time has established himself in his first studio, in the Albert Buildings, 24 Shandwick Place, Edinburgh.

Exhibits for the first time in the Royal Scottish Academy and Royal Glasgow Institute annual exhibitions and continues to do so regularly for the rest of his life.

1897
Exhibits for the first time in the Society of Scottish Artists annual exhibition and continues to do so regularly until 1919 and finally in 1930.

C.1900
Moves studio to 7 Devon Place, Edinburgh.

Begins friendship with Fergusson.

First of several painting trips to Comrie, Perthshire.

1903
First solo exhibition, at The Scottish Gallery, Edinburgh.

Salon d'Automne established in Paris.

1904
Painting trip to Islay with Fergusson.

Summer painting trips to France with Fergusson from now until 1907.

1905
Moves studio to 32 York Place, Edinburgh, built in 1795 for Henry Raeburn.

1907
Exhibits for the first time in London in various group shows, including at the Baillie Gallery, the Goupil Gallery and the first exhibition of the Allied Artists Association.

First work acquired for a public collection when the Scottish Modern Arts Association purchases *Still Life*, *c.*1906 (City Art Centre, Edinburgh).

1909

Fails to be elected an Associate of the Royal Scottish Academy.

Friendship with Cadell has begun by now.

Solo exhibition at The Scottish Gallery, Edinburgh.

Exhibits for the first time at the Venice Biennale (also in 1910, 1924 and 1930).

1910

Marries Margaret Mackay on 5 April at Christ Church, Morningside, Edinburgh.

Paints with Fergusson in Royan, where first son, Willy, born on 29 August.

Moves to studio-apartment at 278 boulevard Raspail, Montparnasse, Paris.

1911

Starts providing illustrations for new periodical *Rhythm* of which Fergusson is Art Editor.

Paints at Ile de Bréhat with Fergusson.

Exhibits for the first time in the Salon d'Automne annual exhibition (also in 1912).

1912

Moves back to Edinburgh.

Rents flat at 13 India Street, which remains the family home until his death.

Takes studio at 34 Queen Street, where he remains until 1917.

Two solo exhibitions at the Stafford Gallery, London.

In group show *Exhibition of Pictures by J.D. Fergusson, A.E. Rice and Others: The Rhythm Group* at the Stafford Gallery, London.

1913

Painting trip to Cassis with Fergusson.

Painting trip to Arran.

Solo exhibition at the New Gallery, 12 Shandwick Place, Edinburgh.

1914

Birth of second son, Denis, on 25 March.

Death of nanny Mary Sanderson on 16 October.

Painting trip to Crawford, Lanarkshire.

Solo exhibition at the Baillie Gallery, London.

In group show *Twentieth-Century Art: A Review of the Modern Movements*, Whitechapel Art Gallery, London.

Start of First World War; declared medically unfit.

1915

First of several painting trips to Kirkcudbright (last is in 1931) and Dumfries & Galloway in general.

First solo exhibition at La Société des Beaux-Arts, Glasgow.

1917

Moves studio to 54 Shandwick Place, where remains until 1934.

1918

Elected an Associate of the Royal Scottish Academy.

Friendship with Hunter has begun by now.

1919

Solo exhibition at La Société des Beaux-Arts, Glasgow.

1920

First painting trip to the Hebridean island of Iona, with Cadell; returns virtually every year until 1935.

1921

Solo exhibition at La Société des Beaux-Arts, Glasgow.

The Scottish Gallery and La Société des Beaux-Arts agree to operate a half-share system with Peploe, splitting sales of his work fifty–fifty.

1922

Solo exhibition at The Scottish Gallery, Edinburgh.

1923

Solo exhibition at The Scottish Gallery, Edinburgh.

In group show *Exhibition of Paintings by S.J. Peploe, F.C.B. Cadell, and Leslie Hunter*, Leicester Galleries, London

1924

Painting trip to Cassis with Cadell.

Solo exhibitions at The Scottish Gallery, Edinburgh and La Société des Beaux-Arts, Glasgow.

In group show *Les Peintres de l'Écosse Moderne: F.C.B. Cadell, J.D. Fergusson, Leslie Hunter and S.J. Peploe*, Galerie Barbazanges, Paris; *Paysage – Iona* is acquired for the French national collection.

1925

In group show *Exhibition of Paintings by S.J. Peploe, Leslie Hunter, F.C.B. Cadell and J.D. Fergusson*, Leicester Galleries, London.

1926

Amalgamation of La Société des Beaux-Arts and the Lefèvre Gallery to form Alex Reid & Lefèvre, with galleries in Glasgow and London.

Solo exhibitions at Reid & Lefèvre in London and Glasgow.

1927

Elected a member of the Royal Scottish Academy.

First work enters British national collection when the Tate Gallery acquires *Tulips* of 1923.

Solo exhibition at The Scottish Gallery, Edinburgh.

1928

Painting trip to Antibes with Hunter and then to Cassis.

Solo exhibition at the C.W. Kraushaar Galleries, New York.

Room dedicated to his work in the *Second Inaugural Loan Exhibition*, Kirkcaldy Museum & Art Gallery.

1929

Painting trip to Boat of Garten in the Highlands.

Solo exhibition at Reid & Lefèvre, London (until January 1930).

1930

Painting trip to Cassis.

Solo exhibition at The Scottish Gallery, Edinburgh.

1931

In group show *Les Peintres Écossais: S.J. Peploe, J.D. Fergusson, Leslie Hunter, F.C.B. Cadell, Telfer Bear, R.O. Dunlop*, Galerie Georges Petit, Paris; *La forêt* is acquired for the French national collection.

Solo exhibition at Reid & Lefèvre, Glasgow.

Death of Hunter on 7 December.

1932

In group show *Paintings by Six Scottish Artists: Peploe, Hunter, Fergusson, Cadell, Bear, Gillies*, Barbizon House, London.

Closure of Reid & Lefèvre's Glasgow gallery; Peploe taken on by Pearson & Westergaard.

1933

First of several painting trips to Calvine, Perthshire.

Joins teaching staff of Edinburgh College of Art; retires the following year due to ill health.

First work acquired for an Australian public collection when *Melon* of *c.*1906 purchased by the Art Gallery of New South Wales.

Death of brother William on 18 March.

1934

Moves to final studio at 65 Castle Street.

Painting trips to St Fillans, Perthshire and Rothiemurchus, Inverness-shire.

Solo exhibitions at The Scottish Gallery, Edinburgh, Reid & Lefèvre, London and Pearson & Westergaard, Glasgow.

1935

Death of brother James on 29 October.

Dies on 11 October at 35 Drumsheugh Gardens, Edinburgh.

1936

Memorial Exhibition at The Scottish Gallery, Edinburgh.

Memorial Displays in the Royal Scottish Academy and Royal Glasgow Institute annual exhibitions.

1937

Memorial Exhibition at the McLellan Galleries, Glasgow, organised by Reid & Lefèvre and Pearson & Westergaard.

Death of Cadell on 6 December.

1939

First work enters Scottish national collection, when J.W. Blyth presents *The Black Bottle* to the National Gallery of Scotland, Edinburgh.

1941

Solo exhibition at the National Gallery of Scotland, Edinburgh.

1943

Death of sister Annie on 22 March.

1947

Publication of *Peploe: An Intimate Memoir of an Artist and of his Work* by Stanley Cursiter.

1953

Touring solo exhibition organised by Denis Peploe with the Scottish Arts Council.

1958

Death of Margaret Peploe on 23 October.

1961

Death of Fergusson on 30 January.

1971

Solo exhibition *S.J. Peploe 1871–1935: Paintings and Drawings from the Collections of Dr R.A. Lillie, OBE, and Aberdeen Art Gallery*, Aberdeen Art Gallery.

1985

Solo exhibition at the Scottish National Gallery of Modern Art, Edinburgh.

1998

Solo exhibition at Kirkcaldy Art Gallery & Museum.

2000

Publication of *S.J. Peploe 1871–1935* by Guy Peploe.

2012

Solo exhibition at St Andrews Museum, St Andrews.

Solo exhibition at the Scottish National Gallery of Modern Art, Edinburgh.

NOTES AND REFERENCES

KEY TO ABBREVIATIONS

NLS
National Library of Scotland

NRS
National Records of Scotland

RGI
Royal Glasgow Institute of the Fine Arts

RSA
Royal Scottish Academy

SNGMA
Scottish National Gallery of Modern Art

SSA
Society of Scottish Artists

[89] Detail from *White Lilies*, mid-1920s [73]

1 · INTRODUCTION · PAGES 11–12

1. P.G. Konody, 'Art gourmet's treat: etchings and paintings at Leicester Galleries', *Daily Mail*, 12 January 1925.

2. *Paintings by Four Scottish Colourists: S.J. Peploe, Leslie Hunter, F.C.B. Cadell, J.D. Fergusson*, T. & R. Annan & Sons Ltd, Glasgow, November 1948.

3. Honeyman was a Director of Reid & Lefèvre from 1929 to 1939. In the latter year he was appointed the first Director of Glasgow Museums and Art Galleries. Honeyman 1950, p.66.

4. Simister 2001, p.23.

5. Fergusson 1962, p.8.

6. Letter from S.J. Peploe to Margaret. Mackay of 9 March 1914, SNGMA, S.J. Peploe Archive.

7. Letter from S.J. Peploe to F.C.B. Cadell of 20 June 1918, NLS, F.C.B. Cadell papers.

8. Honeyman 1950, p.66.

9. Letter from E.A. Taylor to T.J. Honeyman of 13 December 1936, NLS, T.J. Honeyman papers, acc.no.9787/45. See letter from S.J. Peploe to F.C.B. Cadell postmarked 7 August 1918, NLS, F.C.B. Cadell papers, which refers to Hunter.

10. A.J. McNeill Reid as quoted in T.J. Honeyman, *Introducing Leslie Hunter*, London, 1937, p.126.

11. 'The Leicester Galleries', *The Times*, 6 January 1923.

12. 'Art exhibitions: paintings by S.J. Peploe', *Glasgow Herald*, 3 April 1924.

13. As explained by Guy Peploe in a lecture given at St Andrews Museum on 20 June 2012.

14. As explained by Guy Peploe to the author in conversation on 22 December 2011.

15. The first such acquisitions were to the collections of the Art Gallery of New South Wales, Sydney in 1933, the Fitzwilliam Museum, Cambridge in 1910, the French nation in 1924, the National Museum of Northern Ireland in 1932 and Kirkcaldy Museum & Art Gallery in 1926.

2 · A LIFE · PAGES 15–26

1. Cursiter 1947, p.73.

2. Peploe 1928.

3. Peploe is listed in the register of the Académie Julian from November 1891 until April 1892 and from January until April 1894, see Archives de L'Académie Julian, Archives Nationales, Paris, 63AS1. The author is grateful to Jane MacAvock for establishing these facts. See Peploe 1928. It has been suggested that Peploe also attended the Académie Colarossi, see Cursiter 1947, p.4, but no evidence has been found to support this and Peploe himself does not mention it in Peploe 1928.

4. Porter 1945, p.5.

5. Cursiter 1947, p.7.

6. Cursiter 1947, p.8.

7. Cursiter 1947, p.8.

8. Cursiter 1947, p.9.

9. Peploe 2000, pp.14–15.

10. Long and Cumming 2000, p.18.

11. Long and Cumming 2000, p.18.

12. Letter from S.J. Peploe to Margaret Mackay of 12 November 1908, SNGMA, S.J. Peploe Archive.

13. Letter from S.J. Peploe to Margaret Mackay of 2 November 1903, quoted in Peploe 2000, p.21.

14. The Scottish Gallery Day Book 1903, entry no.176, 10 November 1903.

15. Caw 1904, p.349.

16. Cursiter 1947, p.17.

17. Cursiter 1947, p.17.

18. Peploe 2000, p.28.

19. Cursiter 1947, pp.24–5.

20. Peploe 2000, n.13, p.163.

21. The Scottish Gallery Day Book, January 1909 – January 1913, entry no.187.

22. Fergusson 1962, pp.46–7.

23. Letter from S.J. Peploe to Margaret Peploe of April 1911, SNGMA, S.J. Peploe Archive.

24. Letter from S.J. Peploe to Margaret Peploe of April 1911, SNGMA, S.J. Peploe Archive.

25. Thanks to successful exhibition sales, the Peploes were able to purchase the flat for £700 in 1924.

26. Honeyman 1950, p.59.

27. Honeyman 1950, p.59.

28. Margaret Peploe, 'Notes for Mr Cursiter's Book', hand-written notes in leather-bound pad, SNGMA, S.J. Peploe Archive.

29. Letters from S.J. Peploe to F.C.B. Cadell of 20 January 1918 and 2 August 1918, NLS, F.C.B. Cadell papers.

30. Peploe 2000, p.53.

31. Cursiter 1947, p.32.

32. 'The Scottish Society of Artists' Exhibition: Post-Impressionist Pictures', The Scotsman, 13 December 1913.

33. See Frances Fowle, 'Three Scottish Colourists: early patronage of Peploe, Hunter and Cadell', Apollo, vol.CLII, no.464, October 2000, p.27.

34. Cursiter 1947, p.37.

35. Letter from S.J. Peploe to Robert Traill Rose of March 1918 quoted in Honeyman 1950, p.65.

36. See Edinburgh and Leith Post Office Directory: General Directory for the years 1917–18 to 1934–5.

37. Billcliffe 1989, p.51.

38. Undated letter from Margery Porter to T.J. Honeyman, NLS, T.J. Honeyman papers, acc. no.9787/45, mss 2/23/22.

39. Honeyman 1950, p.66.

40. Letter from S.J. Peploe to F.C.B. Cadell of 2 August 1918, see Hewlett and Macmillan 2011, p.80.

41. Letter from F.C.B. Cadell to S.J. Peploe of 7 July 1932, private collection.

42. Cursiter 1947, p.53.

43. Cursiter 1947, pp.71–2.

44. Jessica Christian and Charles Stiller, Iona Portrayed: The Island through Artists' Eyes 1760–1960, Inverness, 2000, p.85. The author is grateful to Mairi MacArthur for her help with research into Iona.

45. The boys included Malcolm Macleod (1922–1982), one of four sons of Captain Malcolm and Martha Macleod who ran the shop in the village and lived at Rosneath Cottage in the main street. The author is grateful to Zoë Macleod for providing this information.

46. As recounted to the author by Mrs Catriona MacNaughton, 26 June 2012.

47. Cursiter 1947, p.86. See Peploe 2000, fig.126, p.160.

48. Honeyman 1950, pp.63–4.

49. Fowle 2010, p.122.

50. Paysage – Iona was acquired in 1924 and La forêt in 1931, both now in the collection of the Musée National d'Art Moderne, Centre Pompidou.

51. Undated letter from S.J. Peploe to J.D. Fergusson, The Fergusson Gallery Archive, Box 10, ref.no.1994.756.

52. 'S.J. Peploe: Kraushaar Galleries', American Art News, 28 January 1928 and letter from Duncan MacDonald to John Kraushaar of 12 April 1928, Kraushaar Galleries records 1885–2006, Archives of American Art, Smithsonian Institution, Washington, Reid & Lefèvre Incoming Correspondence 1928, Box 13.29. The works which sold were Tulips to L.B. Williams of Cleveland for £50 and Roses to John T. Spaulding of Boston, for £90. The author is grateful to Margaret Drew Bongiovanni, Furman University (Greenville, SC; Class of '13) for undertaking research into this archive on her behalf.

53. 'Royal Scottish Academy: a new Academician', Glasgow Herald, 10 February 1927.

54. Peploe 2000, p.84.

55. Cursiter 1947, p.82.

56. Cursiter 1947, p.79.

57. Dean 2a Cemetery, GPR grave number 71728. The author is grateful to Charles Sale of gravestonephotos.com for this information.

58. Will of S.J. Peploe, NRS, SC70/4/713, p.12.

59. David Foggie, 'Peploe's art: a Scotsman under French influence', The Scotsman, 14 October 1935.

60. Margaret Peploe, 'Notes for Mr Cursiter's Book', hand-written notes in leather-bound pad, SNGMA, S.J. Peploe Archive.

61. Cursiter 1947, pp.65–6.

62. As recounted to the author by Mrs Catriona MacNaughton, 26 June 2012.

63. Fergusson 1962, p.11.

64. Letter from Margaret Peploe to J.W. Blyth postmarked 19 May 1939, private collection. See The Taste of J.W. Blyth, exh. cat., The Scottish Gallery, 4–28 July 2012, p.12.

65. Porter 1935.

3 · PEPLOE IN FRANCE
PAGES 43–53

1. Letter from Peploe to Margaret Mackay, Paris-Plage 1907, SNGMA, S.J. Peploe Archive.

2. This was a landscape of Iona. A second landscape (of Cassis) was acquired by the French state in 1931.

3. See Livres de comptabilité des élèves, livre 92, 1890–92, Académie Julian archives, Paris. Peploe is registered in the list of 'élèves recommandés' (where he is described as 'ami de Laing') as living at 8 rue de Grenelle. He later 'recommended' Robert Brough as a potential student.

4. See Atelier Hommes de MM J.P. Laurens et B. Constant, 31 rue du Dragon, Année 1894–1895, Académie Julian archives, Paris. Cursiter 1947, p.5 observes that Peploe also attended the Académie Colarossi, where he won a silver medal in 1894. On Brough see Jennifer Melville, Robert Brough ARSA 1872–1905, Aberdeen, 1995.

5. Letter 14 to Miss Mackay, 19 Rutland Square, 12 Nov 1908 (from Carmel House, Corpach), SNGMA, S.J. Peploe Archive.

6. J.D. Fergusson, 'Memories of Peploe', Scottish Art Review, vol.VIII, no.3, 1962, p.8, reproduced in Morris 2010, p.42.

7. Moore 1893, p.86.

8. Letter dated 4 June 1894 from Peploe to Alfred Terry, SNGMA, S.J. Peploe Archive. (Also reproduced in Peploe 2000, p.13.)

9. In April and May 1894. See MaryAnne Stevens (ed.), Alfred Sisley, exh. cat., Royal Academy of Arts, London, 1992, p.238.

10. For further details see Frances Fowle with essays by Jennifer Melville and Vivien Hamilton, Impressionism and Scotland, exh. cat., National Galleries of Scotland, Edinburgh, 2008, pp.67–70 and Fowle 2010, pp.43–53.

11. According to Elizabeth Cumming, they certainly knew each other by 1900. See Elizabeth Cumming, '"*Les Peintres de l'Écosse Moderne*": the Colourists and France' in Long and Cumming 2000, p.42.

12. Fergusson recorded in his memoirs, 'We were both very much impressed with the Impressionists, whose work we saw in the Salle Caillebotte, and in Durand-Ruel's gallery.' J.D. Fergusson in Morris 2010, p.42.

13. 'Agenda de la semaine', *L'Illustration*, 6 May 1899, cited in MaryAnne Stevens (ed.), *Alfred Sisley*, exh. cat., Royal Academy of Arts, London, 1992, p.281.

14. An example is Sisley's *Rue de la Princesse, Louveciennes*, *c*.1872–3 (Phillips Collection, Washington), which Peploe could have seen at Durand-Ruel's 1899 exhibition. See MaryAnne Stevens (ed.), *Alfred Sisley*, exh. cat., Royal Academy of Arts, London, 1992, p.118.

15. Caw 1904, p.348.

16. In *Modern Painting* (1893) George Moore included a chapter on 'Monet, Sisley, Pissaro [sic] and the Decadence'; also in 1893 Sir George Reid, President of the Royal Scottish Academy delivered a diatribe against the influence of Impressionism on Scottish painting which was published in the *Westminster Gazette* on 4 February 1893. See Frances Fowle with essays by Jennifer Melville and Vivien Hamilton, *Impressionism and Scotland*, exh. cat., National Galleries of Scotland, Edinburgh, 2008, p.21.

17. J.D. Fergusson, 'Memories of Peploe', *Scottish Art Review*, vol.VIII, no.3, 1962, p.8.

18. James Guthrie and John Lavery also visited the exhibition. See Belinda Thomson, 'Patrick Geddes's "Clan d'Artistes": some elusive French connections' in F. Fowle and B. Thomson (eds), *Patrick Geddes: The French Connection*, Oxford, 2004, pp.55–6 and n.21. See also review by Camille Mauclair in the *Art Journal*, 1895, pp.274–9.

19. George Moore, *Modern Painting*, London, 1893, pp.33, 36–8, 42.

20. Ibid., pp.36–7.

21. He seems also to have been inspired by the pose of Alexis Grimou's (1678–1733) *The Toper* (Scottish National Gallery, Edinburgh).

22. A three-quarter-length portrait of a woman in walking costume, this was exhibited as *La Jeune Fille au Fichu* (*The Scotsman*, 14 July 1900, p.8).

23. Reid appears to have acquired the *Portrait of Victorine Meurent* from the dealer Gustave Tempelaere and sold it to William Burrell on 22 April 1901 for £4,000. For details of this transaction see Fowle 2010, p.52 and n.95, p.164. In 1899 Reid also sold a head-and-shoulders pastel of an unknown woman to the Glasgow collector Andrew Kirkpatrick. Peploe visited Reid's gallery in February 1901 with Charles Hodge Mackie. See Fowle 2010, p.118.

24. D.S. MacColl, *Nineteenth-Century Art*, Glasgow, 1902, p.151.

25. Ibid.

26. For example, works such as Manet's *Still Life: Fruit on a Table* of 1864 (Musée d'Orsay, Paris), which he could have seen at Bernheim-Jeune's gallery in Paris in 1901.

27. J.D. Fergusson in Morris 2010, p.45.

28. Jane Quigley, 'Picardy, a quiet, simple land', *The Craftsman*, vol.XII, no.3, 1907, p.256.

29. On these artists and their French connections, see Frances Fowle, 'The Franco-Scottish Alliance: artistic links between Scotland and France in the late 1880s and 1890s' and Belinda Thomson, 'Patrick Geddes's "Clan d'Artistes": some elusive French connections', in in F. Fowle and B. Thomson (eds), *Patrick Geddes: The French Connection*, Oxford, 2004, esp. pp.31–3 and 52–60.

30. Russell T. Clement, *Les Fauves: A Sourcebook*, Westport, 1994, pp.xxvii–xxviii.

31. He had solo exhibitions in November 1907, December–January 1908–9 and April 1910.

32. Russell T. Clement, *Les Fauves: A Sourcebook*, Westport, 1994, p.564.

33. *The Times*, 12 October 1908, p.4.

34. This was in 1911.

35. J.D. Fergusson in Morris 2010, pp.46–7.

36. For more on this circle of artists, and especially Fergusson's period in Paris, see Elizabeth Cumming, '"*Les Peintres de l'Écosse Moderne*": the Colourists and France' in Long and Cumming 2000, pp.41–55; and Elizabeth Cumming, 'Colour, rhythm and dance: the paintings and drawings of J.D. Fergusson and his circle', in Cumming 1985, pp.6–12. See also Ysanne Holt, *British Artists and the Modernist Landscape*, Aldershot, 2003, chapter 4 'Landscapes and rhythm', pp.81–94.

37. Morris 2010, p.47.

38. On *Rhythm* see Faith Binckes, *Modernism, Magazines and the British Avant-Garde: Reading Rhythm, 1910–1914*, Oxford, 2010 and Sheila McGregor, 'J.D. Fergusson and the periodical *Rhythm*' in Cumming 1985, pp.13–17.

39. Peploe contributed to the following editions: vol.1, no.1 (summer 1911), *Study*, p.19; *Gate of the Luxembourg Gardens*, p.23; vol.1, no.2 (autumn 1911), *Place de l'Observatoire*, p.25; vol.1, no.3 (winter 1911), *Study*, p.3; *Study*, p.27; vol.1, no.4 (spring 1912), *Drawing*, p.6; *Drawing*, p.20; *Drawing*, p.33; vol. 2, no.6 (1912–07) *Study*, p.44; vol.2, no.9 (1912–10) *Head*, p.188; *Head*, p.206; *Drawing*, p.217; *Head*, p.227; vol.2, no.10 (1912–11) *Nude Study*, p.264; *Drawing*, p.273; vol.2, no.11 (1912–12) *Drawing*, p.326.

40. Fry's formalist theory was first articulated in 'An essay in aesthetics', published in the *New Quarterly* in April 1909. He also published a translation of Maurice Denis's text on Cézanne in the *Burlington Magazine* in January 1910, where Denis discusses Cézanne's compositions in terms of a 'plane surface covered with colours arranged in a determined order'. See Maurice Denis, 'Cézanne' (translated by Roger Fry), *Burlington Magazine*, January 1910, p.276.

41. John Middleton Murry, 'Art and Philosophy', *Rhythm*, vol.1, 1911, p.12.

42. Ibid.

43. Henri Bergson, *Time and Free Will: An Essay on the Immediate Data of Consciousness* (1888), London, 1910, pp.12–16. Murry's 'rhythm' was also associated with the notion of *élan vital* as outlined in Bergson's *Creative Evolution*, published in English in 1911. On this see Mark Antliff, *Inventing Bergson: Cultural Politics and the Parisian Avant-Garde*, Princeton, 1993, pp.67–105.

44. Michael T.H. Sadler, 'Fauvism and a Fauve', *Rhythm*, vol.1, 1911, p.17. This text was originally published in *L'Occident* in September 1907. Sadler later spelled his surname 'Sadleir' to avoid confusion with his father, also Michael Sadler.

45. P.G. Konody, 'Rhythm', *The Observer*, 16 July 1911, p.11, cited in Faith Binckes, *Modernism, Magazines and the British Avant-Garde: Reading Rhythm, 1910–1914*, Oxford, 2010, p.77.

46. Letter dated 13 December 1939 from E.A. Taylor to T.J. Honeyman, cited in Peploe 2000, p.47. Chabaud had moved to Paris in 1907 and exhibited at the Salon d'Automne that year and again in 1909, when Fergusson praised his work in a piece for *Art Review*.

47. *Outlook*, 25 November 1911, p.739, cited in J.B. Bullen (ed.), *Post-Impressionists in England: The Critical Reception,* London, 1988, p.25.

48. Review in the *Morning Post*, cited in Martin Bailey with an essay by Frances Fowle, *Van Gogh and Britain: Pioneer Collectors*, exh. cat., National Galleries of Scotland, Edinburgh, 2006, p.22.

49. Ibid.

50. Frances Fowle, 'Following the vision: from Brittany to Edinburgh', in Belinda Thomson with essays by Frances Fowle and Lesley Stevenson, *Gauguin's Vision*, exh. cat., National Galleries of Scotland, Edinburgh, 2005, pp.104–6.

51. Peploe 2000, p.48. A total of thirty-five pictures were supplied by The Scottish Gallery, who continued to act as Peploe's agent.

52. Review in the *Morning Post*, 19 February 1912, quoted in Peploe 2000, p.48.

53. Roger Fry, Introduction to catalogue *Manet and the Post-Impressionists*, 1910, reproduced in Christopher Reed (ed.), *A Roger Fry Reader*, Chicago and London, 1996, p.85.

54. Cited in Anna Gruetzner Robins, *Modern Art in Britain 1910–1914*, London, 1996, p.108.

55. P.G. Konody, 'Art and artists: English Post-Impressionists', *The Observer*, 27 October 1912, p.10, cited in J.B. Bullen (ed.), *Post-Impressionists in England: The Critical Reception,* London, 1988, p.386.

56. Extract from the *Daily Chronicle*, 16 October 2012, cited in Peploe 2000, p.49. See also Anna Gruetzner Robins, *Modern Art in Britain 1910–1914*, London, 1996, p.113.

57. Specifically the reviewers for the *Morning Post* and the *The Standard*. Peploe 2000, p.49.

58. Extract from the *Daily Chronicle*, 16 October 2012, cited in Peploe 2000, p.49. See also Anna Gruetzner Robins, *Modern Art in Britain 1910–1914*, London, 1996, p.113.

59. He had moved into a new studio at 34 Queen Street, Edinburgh, by June 1912.

60. Peploe 2000, p.50

61. 'Studio-talk', *The Studio*, vol.61, 1914, p.232.

62. Peploe 2000, pp.68 and 70.

63. Ibid., p.74.

64. Ibid., pp.75 and 76.

65. T.M. Wood, 'Art Notes', *Colour*, vol.1, no.1, August 1914, p.8, cited in Faith Binckes, *Modernism, Magazines and the British Avant-Garde: Reading Rhythm, 1910–1914*, Oxford, 2010, p.77.

4 · THE POST-WAR PAINTINGS
PAGES 67–72

1. Review in the *Pall Mall Gazette*, 29 June 1912, of an exhibition of drawings by Peploe at the Stafford Gallery, London.

2. 'Virile Pictures at the Stafford Gallery', *Evening Standard*, 9 October 1912. *The Sunday Times*, 13 October 1912 recorded that 'while J.D. Fergusson and Joseph Simpson paint because they haven't been endowed with a keen vision and a deft brain', Peploe 'paints ... because he is forced to by the strength of the feelings stirring within'.

3. Fry, 'Acquisition by the National Gallery at Helsingfors', *Burlington Magazine*, February 1911, p.293; republished in Christopher Reed (ed.), *A Roger Fry Reader*, Chicago and London, 1996, pp.136–7.

4. Fowle 2010, p.119.

5. Fowle 2010, p.122.

6. Ion Harrison, 'As I remember them', in Honeyman 1950, p.119.

7. This work has previously been dated to *c*.1916, but it is so closely related to the work that Cadell made immediately after the war, when he was working very closely with Peploe, that a date of *c*.1919 is suggested here.

8. Cursiter 1947, pp.83–4.

9. Honeyman 1950, p.45.

10. Sir Claude Phillips in the *Daily Telegraph*, 23 January 1923.

11. *Morning Post*, 16 January 1923.

12. P.G.Konody, 'Scottish painters: the work of three colourists', *Daily Mail*, 9 January 1923.

13. Writing home to Margaret, S.J. Peploe commented that they both felt 'heavy as lead after it', SNGMA, S.J. Peploe Archive.

14. The painting would be joined by three further Colourist purchases in 1931: Peploe's *The Forest*, Fergusson's *River Goddess* and Leslie Hunter's *Loch Lomond*.

15. The reference in the Biennale listing is to a 'J.C. Peploe' which was probably an error. Peploe had already shown there in 1909 and 1910, Cadell in 1914, Fergusson in 1909 and 1912.

16. W.R. Sickert, preface to the catalogue of the *Exhibition of Paintings by S.J. Peploe, Leslie Hunter, F.C.B. Cadell and J.D. Fergusson*, Ernest Brown & Phillips, The Leicester Galleries, Leicester Square, London, 1925.

17. A.L.B. 1927.

18. R.R. Tatlock in the *Daily Telegraph*, 7 December 1929.

19. *The Scotsman*, 9 December 1929.

20. See Margery Porter's account of her visits to the studio in the 1920s, NLS, T.J. Honeyman papers, acc.no.9787/45, MSS 2/23/22.

21. Rutter's review in the *Sunday Times* was of the 68th annual exhibition of the RGI held at the McLellan Galleries.

22. Letter of 31 January 1935 to Florence Drummond, a friend of his late brother: quoted in Peploe 2000, p.60.

5 · PEPLOE SINCE 1935
PAGES 97–99

1. James L. Caw, *Scottish Painting Past and Present*, 1908, p.452.

2. *Morning Post*, 27 April 1936.

3. Honeyman 1935.

4. Caw 1936.

5. Foggie 1935.

6. J.W. Blyth in *The Scotsman*, 11 May 1936, p.13.

7. See Pam Beasant (ed.), *Stanley Cursiter: A Life of the Artist*, Orkney, 2007, p.70.

8. Long and Cumming 2000.

9. Peploe 2000.

10. Fergusson 1962.

11. Cumming 1985.

12. Roger Fry on Paul Cézanne, *The Nation*, 3 December 1910, pp.402–3.

SELECT BIBLIOGRAPHY

BOOKS AND JOURNALS

A.L.B. 1927
A.L.B., 'London notes' (review of S.J. Peploe exhibition at Reid & Lefèvre, London), *The Studio,* vol.93, 1927, pp.119–20

BILLCLIFFE 1989
Roger Billcliffe, *The Scottish Colourists,* London, 1989

BLAIKIE MURDOCH 1910
W.G. Blaikie Murdoch, 'S.J. Peploe: an appreciation', *Memories of Swinburne and Other Essays,* Edinburgh, 1910, pp.36–43

CAW 1904
J.L. Caw, 'Studio talk – Edinburgh', *The Studio,* vol.30, 1904, pp.161 and 346–8

CAW 1936
James L. Caw, 'Foreword', *Memorial Exhibition of Eighty-Three Paintings by S.J. Peploe RSA,* exh. cat., The Scottish Gallery, Edinburgh, 1936

CHRISTIAN AND STILLER 2000
Jessica Christian and Charles Stiller, *Iona Portrayed: The Island through Artists' Eyes 1760–1960,* Inverness, 2000

CUMMING 1985
Elizabeth Cumming et al*., Colour, Rhythm and Dance: Paintings and Drawings by J.D. Fergusson and his Circle in Paris,* exh. cat., Scottish Arts Council touring exhibition, Edinburgh, 1985

CURSITER 1947
Stanley Cursiter, *Peploe: An Intimate Memoir of the Artist and his Work,* Edinburgh, 1947

FERGUSSON 1962
J.D. Fergusson, 'Memories of Peploe', *Scottish Art Review,* vol.VIII, no.3, 1962, pp.8–12 & 31–2

FOGGIE 1935
David Foggie, 'Peploe's art', *The Scotsman,* 14 October 1935

FOGGIE 1937
David Foggie, 'S.J. Peploe RSA', *Outlook,* vol.1, no.10, January 1937, pp.46–50

FOWLE 2010
Frances Fowle, *Van Gogh's Twin: The Scottish Art Dealer Alexander Reid 1854–1928,* Edinburgh, 2010

GORDON 2008
Haig Gordon, *Tales of the Kirkcudbright Artists,* Kirkcudbright, 2008

HERALD 1935
Glasgow Herald, Obituary of S.J. Peploe, 14 October 1935

HEWLETT AND MACMILLAN 2011
Tom Hewlett and Duncan Macmillan, *F.C.B. Cadell: The Life and Works of a Scottish Colourist 1883–1937,* London, 2011

HONEYMAN 1935
T.J. Honeyman, 'Artists of note, number ten: S.J. Peploe RSA', *The Artist,* December 1935, pp.121–4

HONEYMAN 1950
T.J. Honeyman, *Three Scottish Colourists,* London, 1950

LONG AND CUMMING 2000
Philip Long and Elizabeth Cumming, *The Scottish Colourists 1900–1930,* exh. cat., Scottish National Gallery of Modern Art, Edinburgh and Royal Academy, London, 2000

MACMILLAN 2001
Duncan Macmillan, *Scottish Arts in the 20th Century, 1890–2001,* Edinburgh, 2001

MORRIS 2010
Margaret Morris, *The Art of J.D. Fergusson: A Biased Biography*, Glasgow, 1974 (2010 edition)

PEPLOE 1928
S.J. Peploe, 'Autobiography', *Exhibition of Paintings by S.J. Peploe*, exh. cat., C.W. Kraushaar Art Galleries, New York, 1928

PEPLOE 1953
Denis Peploe, 'S.J. Peploe', *S.J. Peploe 1871–1935*, Edinburgh, 1953

PEPLOE 1985
Guy Peploe, *S.J. Peploe 1871–1935*, exh. cat., Scottish National Gallery of Modern Art, Edinburgh, 1985

PEPLOE 2000
Guy Peploe, *S.J. Peploe 1871–1985*, Edinburgh, 2000

PORTER 1935
F.P. Porter, 'An appreciation: S.J. Peploe', *The Scotsman*, 15 October 1935

PORTER 1945
Frederick Porter, 'The art of S.J. Peploe', *The New Alliance*, December 1945 to January 1946, vol.VI, no.6

RHYTHM
Rhythm, illustrations by S.J. Peploe in vol.1, nos 1–4, 1911–12 and vol.2, nos 6, 9–11, 1912

SCOTSMAN 1935
The Scotsman, Obituary of S.J. Peploe, 14 October 1935

SICKERT 1925
Walter Sickert, 'Preface', *Exhibition of Paintings by S.J. Peploe, Leslie Hunter, F.C.B. Cadell and J.D. Fergusson*, exh. cat., Leicester Galleries, London, 1925

SIMISTER 2001
Kirsten Simister, *Living Paint: J.D. Fergusson 1874–1961*, Edinburgh, 2001

SMITH AND MARRINER 2012
Bill Smith and Jill Marriner, *Hunter Revisited: The Life and Art of Leslie Hunter*, Edinburgh, 2012

STRANG 2011
Alice Strang, *F.C.B. Cadell*, exh. cat., Scottish National Gallery of Modern Art, Edinburgh, 2011

TAYLOR 1924
E.A. Taylor, 'S.J. Peploe ARSA', *The Studio*, vol.87, 1924, pp.63–4

TAYLOR 1937
E.A. Taylor, 'Foreword', *Memorial Exhibition of Paintings by S. J. Peploe RSA*, exh. cat., McLellan Galleries, Glasgow, 1937

TIMES 1935
The Times, Obituary of S.J. Peploe, 16 October 1935

TONGE 1938
John Tonge, *The Arts of Scotland*, London, 1938

ARCHIVES

Archives of American Art, Smithsonian Institution, Washington: Kraushaar Galleries Records 1885–2006

Edinburgh College of Art Archive

The Fergusson Gallery Archive, Perth

Glasgow University Special Collections: Jessie M. King and E.A. Taylor Papers, MS Gen 1654

National Library of Scotland, Edinburgh: F.C.B. Cadell papers, acc.no.1124/1; T.J. Honeyman papers, acc.no.9787/45; two sketchbooks by S.J. Peploe, Dep.297 and papers of A.J. McNeill Reid, Esq., acc.no.6925/II P

National Records of Scotland, Edinburgh: Wills of Robert Luff Peploe, SC70/4/210/302-15 and of S.J. Peploe, SC70/4/713/12

Royal Scottish Academy Archive, Edinburgh

Scottish National Gallery of Modern Art Archive, Edinburgh: S.J. Peploe Archive, GMA A112; S.J. Peploe exhibition, National Gallery of Scotland, 1941, GMA A33/1/2/01; S.J. Peploe exhibition, Scottish National Gallery of Modern Art, 1985, GMA A33/1/2/130; plus F.C.B. Cadell Archives on loan from three private collections, GMA AL/16, GMA AL/20 and GMA AL/21

The Scottish Gallery Archive, Edinburgh

The Stewartry Museum Archive, Kirkcudbright

Tate Archive, London: Alex Reid & Lefèvre Ltd Papers, TGA 200211

ACKNOWLEDGEMENTS

In addition to those thanked in the Directors' Foreword, we are grateful to the following people who have helped with this publication and the exhibition and displays which it accompanies: Faith and Joshua Archer; Athina Athanasiadou and Emily Walsh, Bourne Fine Art, Edinburgh; John G. Bernasconi, University of Hull; Lt. Col. R.J. Binks, Scottish National War Memorial, Edinburgh; Sharon Bromberger; Rosina Buckland, George Dalgleish and Michelle Forster-Davies, National Museums Scotland; Mungo Campbell and Elizabeth Jacklin, Hunterian Art Gallery, Glasgow; Griffin Co and Ann Steed, Aberdeen Art Gallery; Jennifer Cooper; Alexander M.D. Corcoran, Lefevre Fine Art, London; Janice Crane and Jane Freel, Kirkcaldy Museum & Art Gallery; Nick Curnow, Linda Robinson and Gavin Strang, Lyon & Turnbull; Jenny Cutts and Robert H.J. Urquhart, National Records of Scotland; Christopher Dawson and Jonathan Horwich, Bonhams; Sue Dearden and Stephen Marquardt, Doughty Hanson & Co; Eleanor Dilloway and Simon Edsor, The Fine Art Society, London and Edinburgh; Richard Emerson; Adrian Glew, Tate Archive; Sally Harrower, National Library of Scotland; Jenny Kinnear, The Fergusson Gallery, Perth; Marie-Claude Lavaly, Musée Municipal de Cassis; Mairi MacArthur; Dr Ellen McAdam, Julie Taylor and Jean Walsh, Glasgow Life; Doug MacBeath, Lloyds Banking Group Archives and Museum; Ishbel Mackinnon and Amy Porteous, University of Edinburgh; Mary Kate MacKinnon; Mark Medcalf, Mark Medcalf Associates; Alexander Meddowes; Rebecca Milner, Manchester Art Gallery; Jean Milton, The Potteries Museum & Art Gallery, Stoke-on-Trent; Susan Morris, Richard Green Gallery, London; David Patterson and Ian O'Riordan, City Art Centre, Edinburgh; David Roberts, Studio SP Ltd; Anna Robertson, The McManus: Dundee's Art Gallery & Museum; Colin and Pauline Saul, The Greengate, Kirkcudbright; Kirsten Simister, Ferens Art Gallery, Hull; Inge and Peter Sloan; Bill Smith; Mark Smith, The Royal Artillery Museum, London; Dr Joanna Soden and Sandy Wood, Royal Scottish Academy, Edinburgh; Patricia Strang; Elizabeth Wemyss and Tommy Zyw, The Scottish Gallery, Edinburgh; George Woods, McLean Museum & Art Gallery, Greenock. We are also grateful to all those who have contributed to the Peploe Project who wish to remain anonymous.